DUBLIN

STREET
& ATLAS
GUID

D1493814

CONTENTS

Scale of maps is 1:15,000 (4.2 inches to 1 mile)

0	0.5	1	1.5km

0	0.25	0.5	0.75	1 mile

LEGEND

Motorway	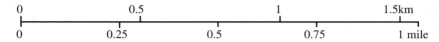	Parks & Playing Fields	
Main Roads/Streets	DAME STREET	Water	
Other Roads/Streets	WILLOW STREET / WILLOW DRIVE	Public Buildings	
Pedestrianised Streets	HENRY STREET	Railway Line	
Built-up Areas		Railway Station	

The maps on pages 4 to 41 are based upon the Ordnance Survey by permission of the Government of the Republic of Ireland.

Printed by The Universities Press (Belfast) Ltd.

Edited by Paul Slevin. Comments, suggestions and inquiries should be addressed to him at the address below. Published by Causeway Press (N.I.), 17 Osborne Park, Bangor, N.Ireland BT20 3DJ. Phone UK 07768 172442. E-mail paulslevin@talk21.com

DISTRIBUTION: Distributed by Eason Wholesale Books (Phone Dublin 862 2111) and Argosy Libraries Ltd (Phone Dublin 806 8460). Quote ISBN 1 872600 73 5

ACKNOWLEDGMENTS: Special thanks go to Catherine Coyle for her help and endurance.

D U B L I N

STREET ATLAS & GUIDE

We all like to kill two birds with one stone, so to speak, but the Dublin Street Atlas & Guide is that extremely rare bird which offers several different products for the price of one.

Firstly, it is a street atlas of the greater Dublin area, based on the latest Ordnance Survey. These maps, together with separate rail and bus maps, will help you to navigate your way through and around the city.

Secondly, it is a detailed guide to the best of what Dublin has to offer. Whether you are visiting for the first time or have lived here all your life, our aim is to help you make the most of this vibrant and colourful city.

The guide is written and published in Ireland, and is based on contributions from people who have immersed themselves in the Dublin social scene with scant regard to their need of sleep or the health of their livers. Having said that, we are always keen to hear alternative views. If you have any recommendations to make or any contrary views to express regarding any of our choices, please write, or e-mail to the addresses given on the page opposite. Any contributions which we use in the future will be acknowledged and a copy of the next edition will be sent in return for the best letters.

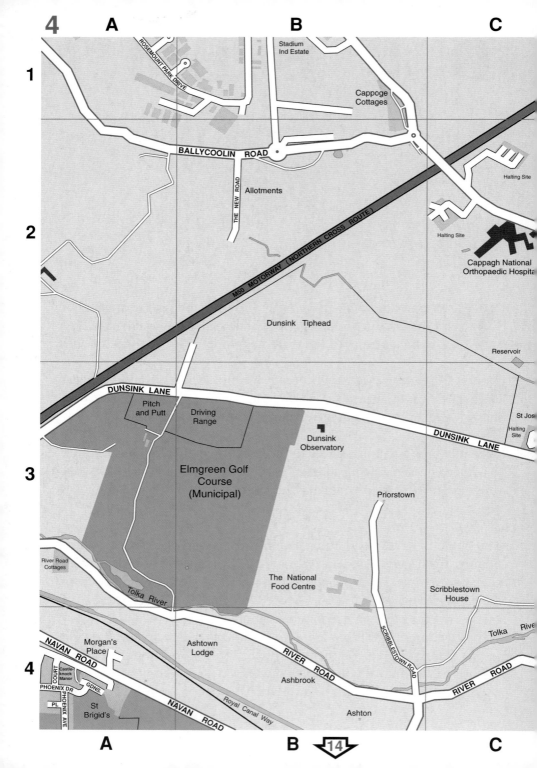

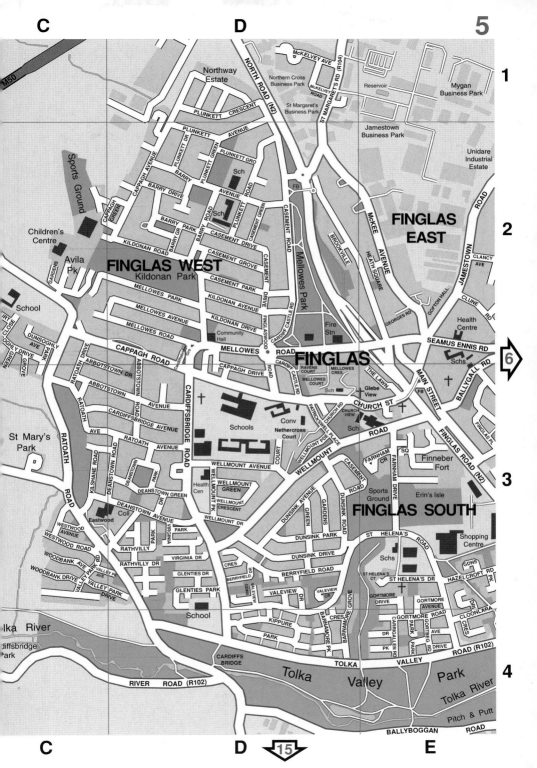

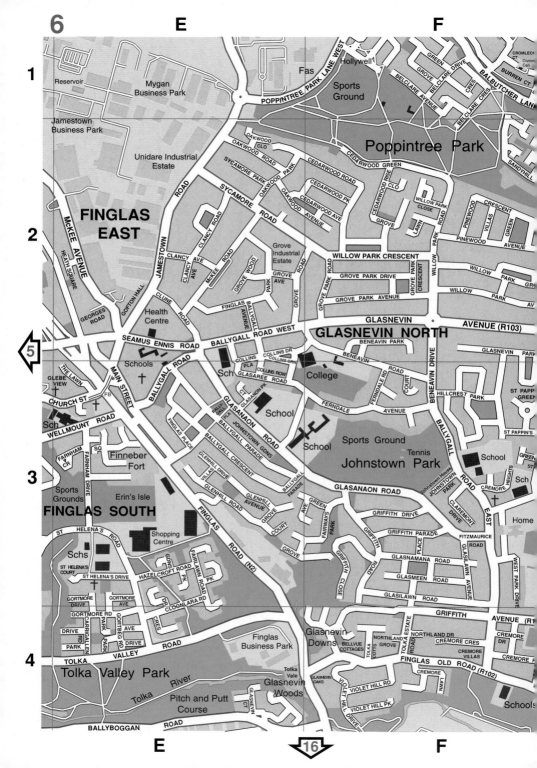

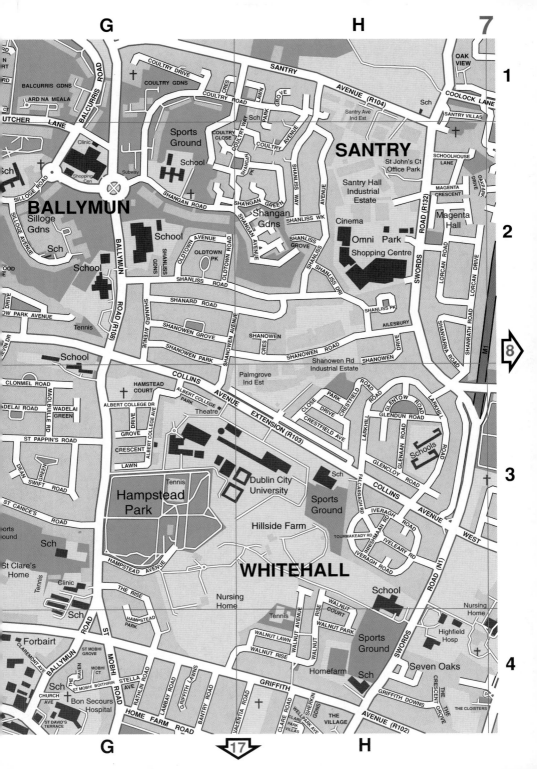

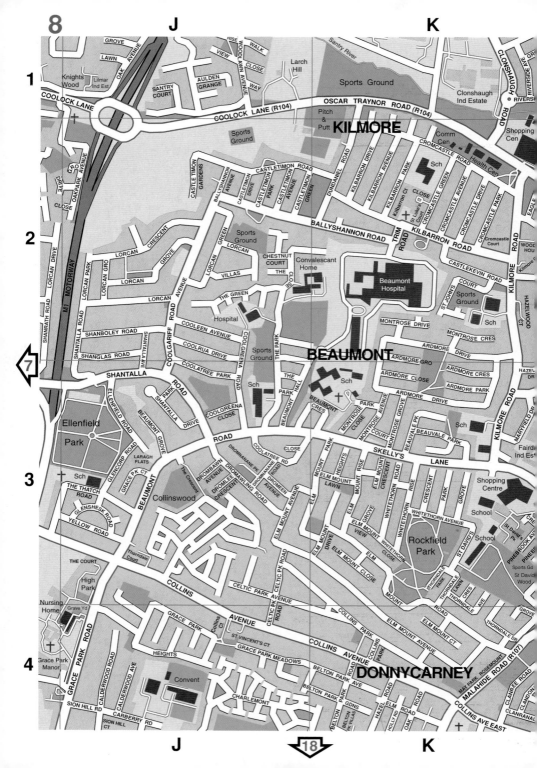

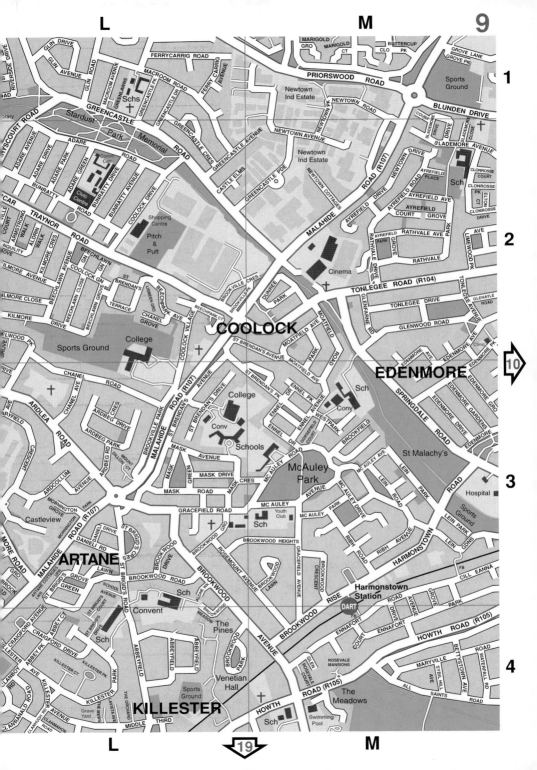

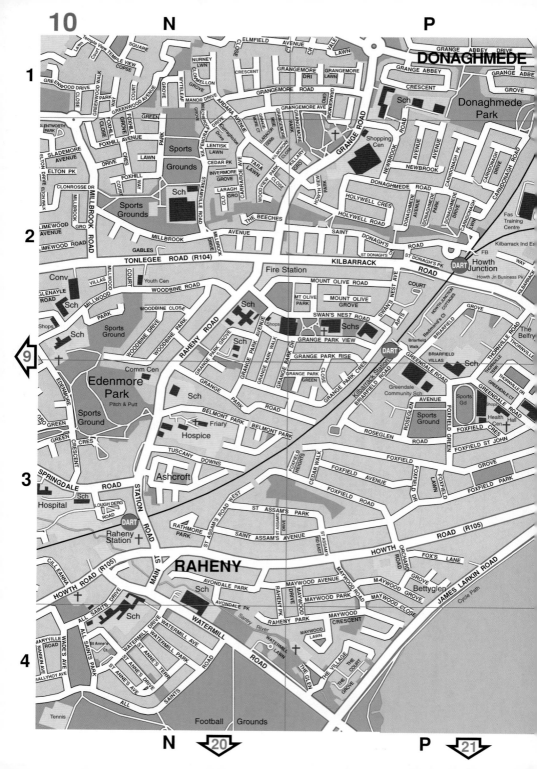

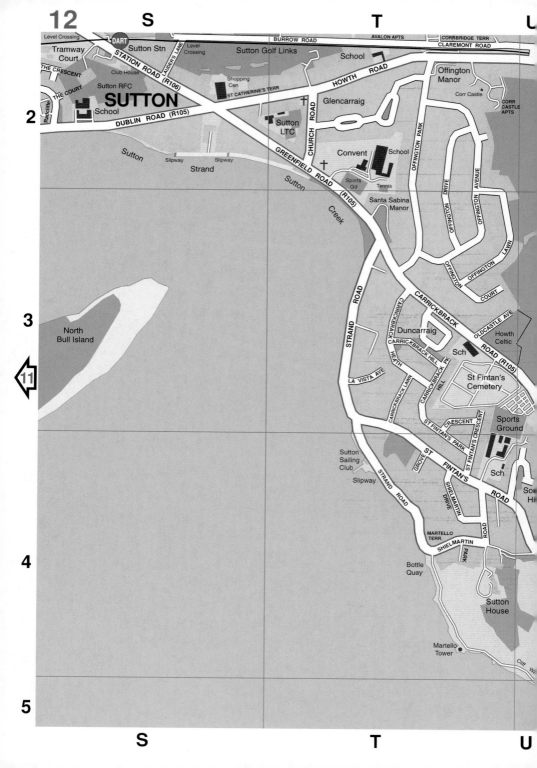

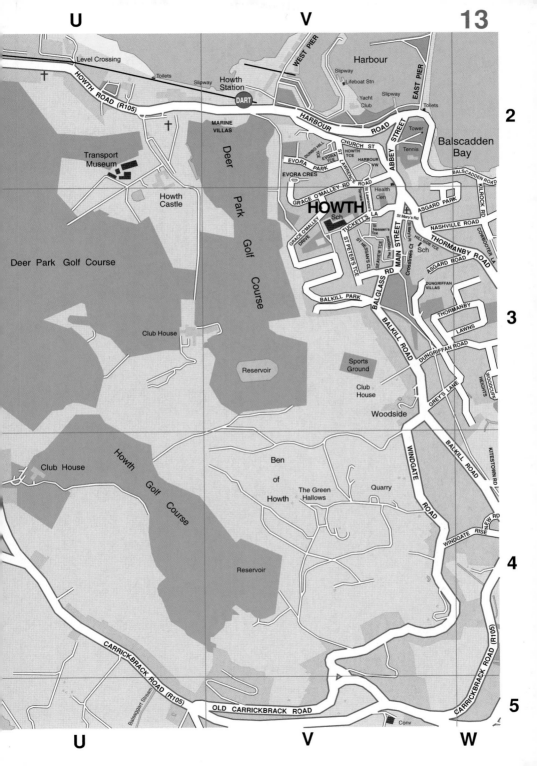

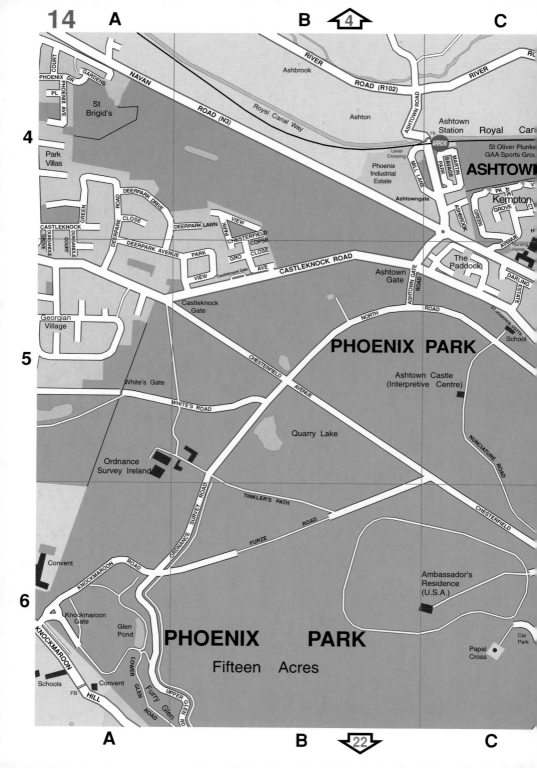

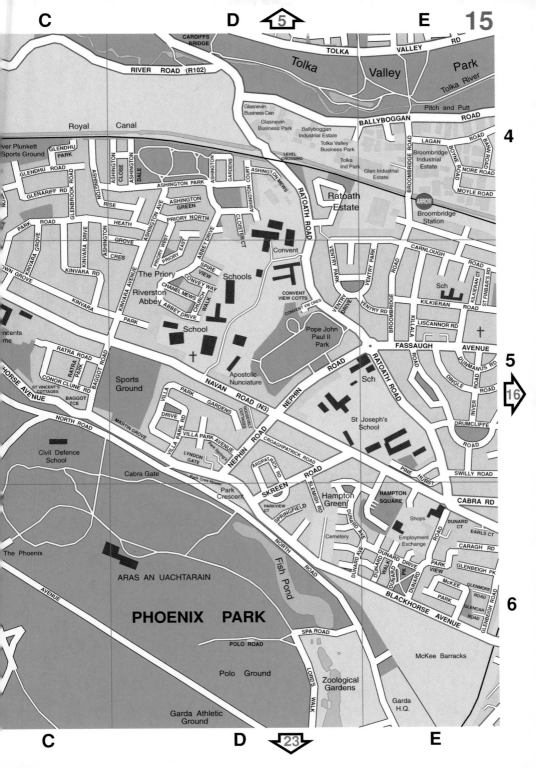

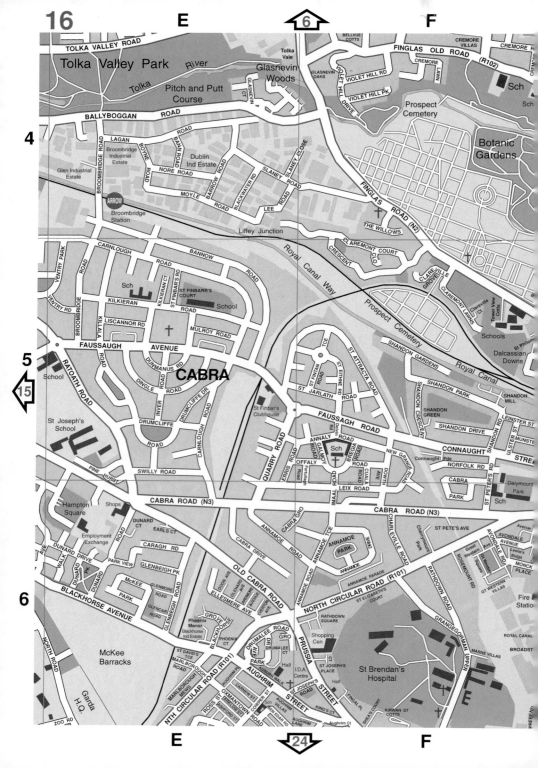

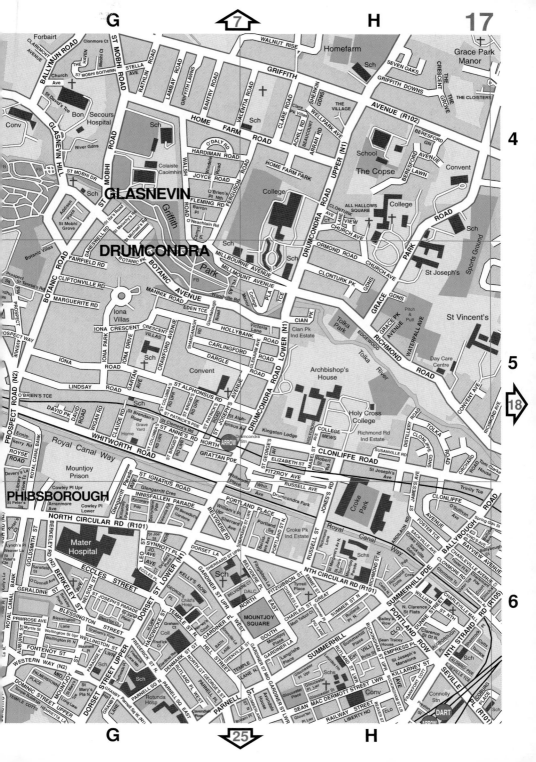

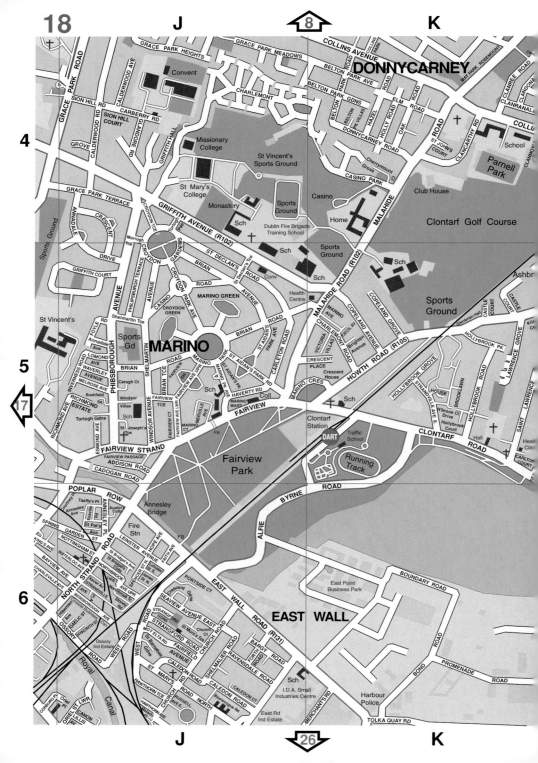

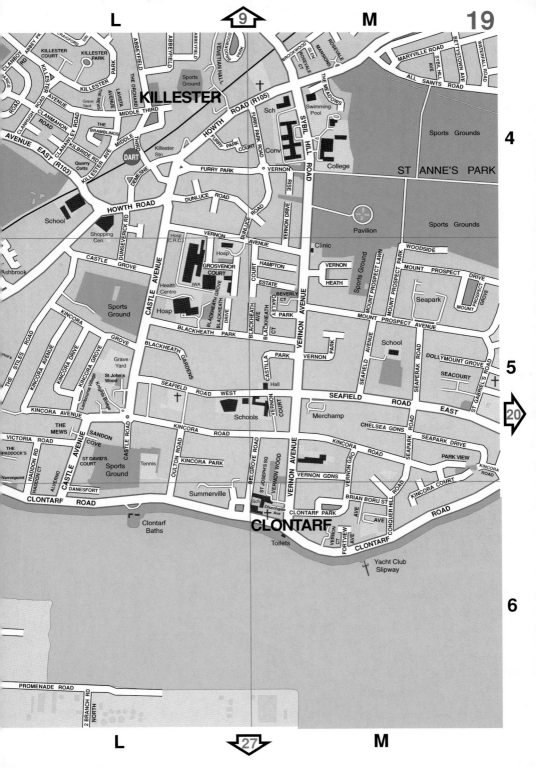

ST ASSAM'S PK
ASSAM'S AVENUE
ROAD (R105)
ST ASSAMS RD E
HOWTH
ORCHARD ROAD
FOX'S LANE
JAMES LARKIN ROAD
3

MAYWOOD AVENUE
MAYWOOD GROVE
MAY WOOD GROVE
GROVE
Cycle Path
MAYWOOD DRIVE
MAYWOOD PARK
MAYWOOD ROAD
MAYWOOD CLO.
Bettyglen

NY PARK
MAYWOOD CRES

MAYWOOD LAWN

THE GLEN
THE VILLAGE
THE GROVE
THE COURT

Nature Reserve

Club House

Car Park
JAMES LARKIN ROAD
CAUSEWAY ROAD
ISLAND
St Anne's Golf Links
4

Nature Reserve

BULL

Nature Reserve
Interpretive Centre

NORTH

Beach

Royal Dublin Golf Links
Nature Reserve
5

Dollymount

6

P   Q

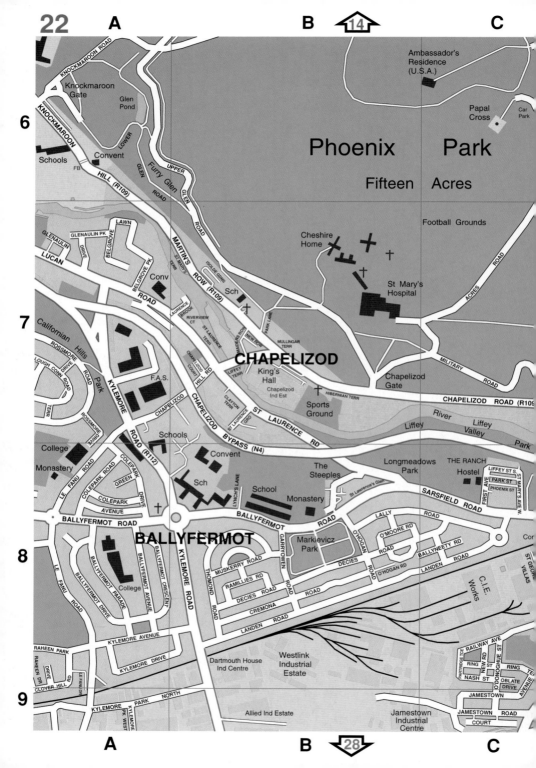

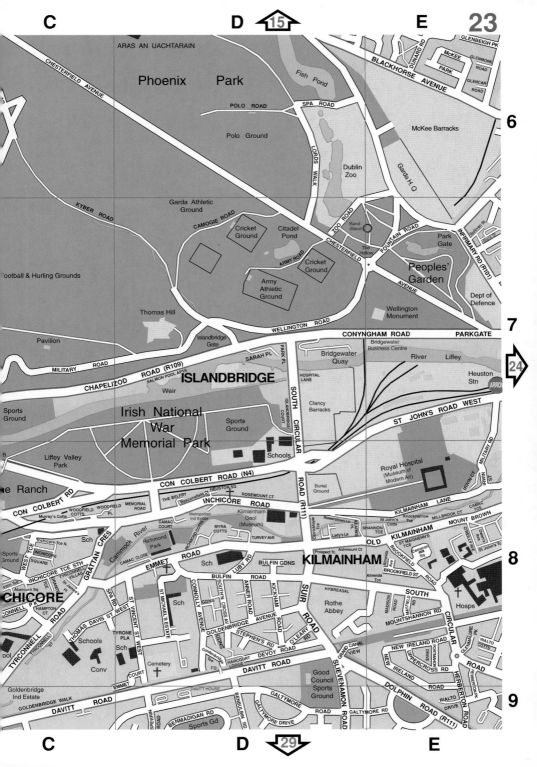

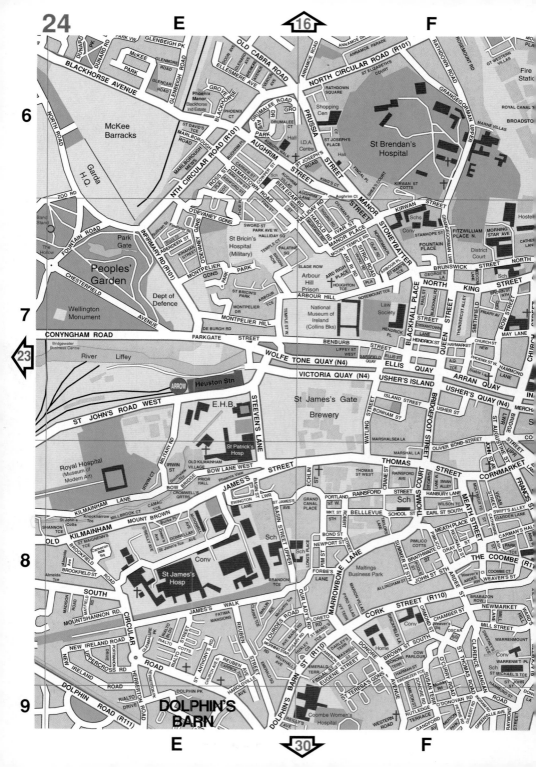

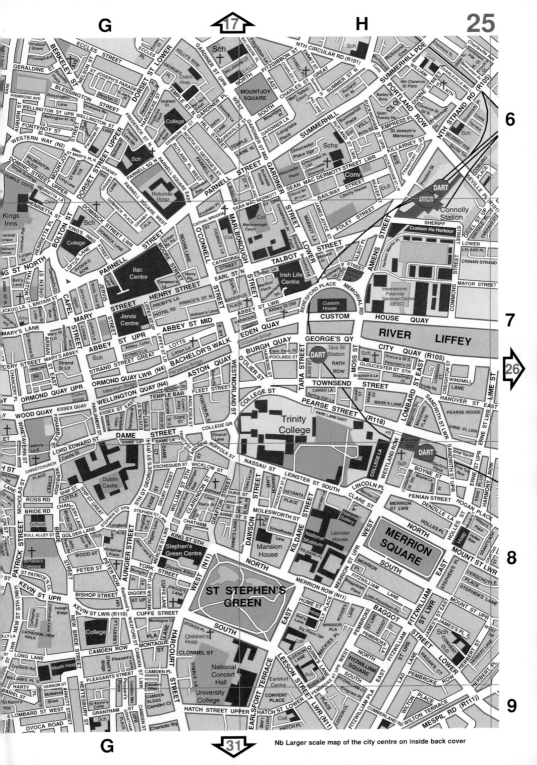

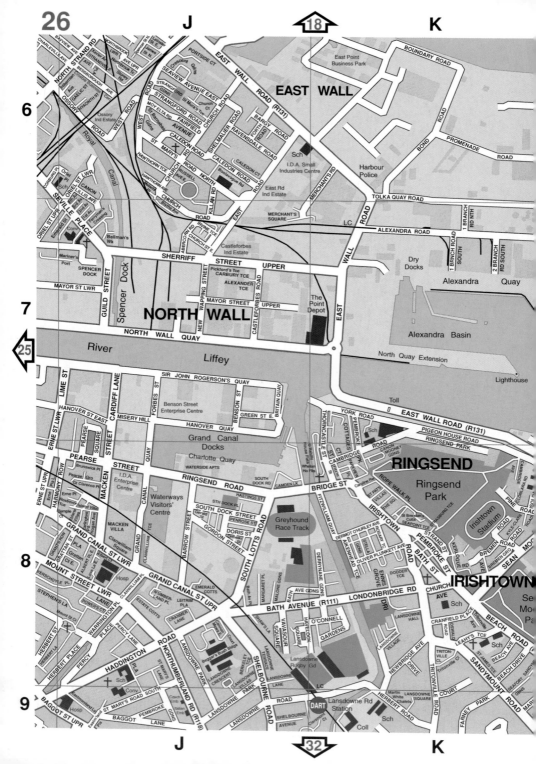

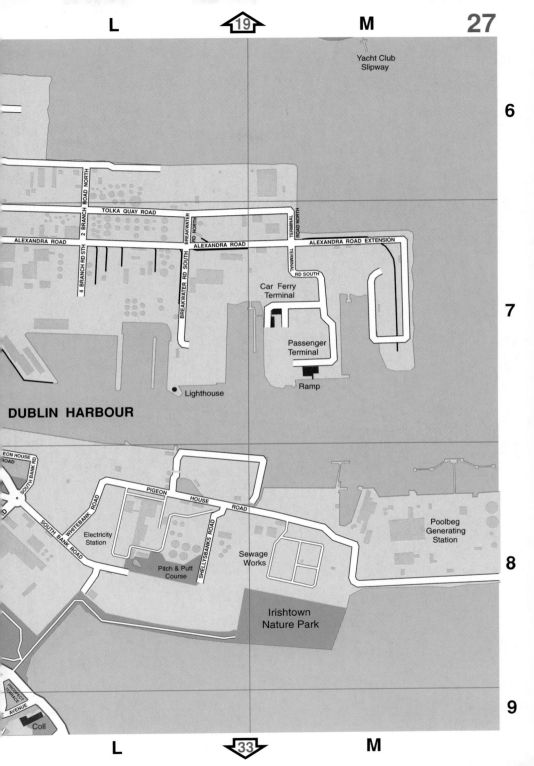

6

Yacht Club
Slipway

2 BRANCH ROAD NORTH

TOLKA QUAY ROAD

BREAKWATER RD NORTH

TERMINAL ROAD NORTH

ALEXANDRA ROAD

ALEXANDRA ROAD

ALEXANDRA ROAD EXTENSION

4 BRANCH RD STH

BREAKWATER RD SOUTH

TERMINAL RD SOUTH

Car Ferry
Terminal

7

Passenger
Terminal

Ramp

Lighthouse

DUBLIN HARBOUR

EON HOUSE
ROAD

SOUTH BANK RD

PIGEON HOUSE ROAD

WHITEBANK ROAD

SOUTH BANK ROAD

SHELLYBANKS ROAD

Electricity
Station

Pitch & Putt
Course

Sewage
Works

Poolbeg
Generating
Station

8

Irishtown
Nature Park

PROSPECT

AVENUE

Coll

9

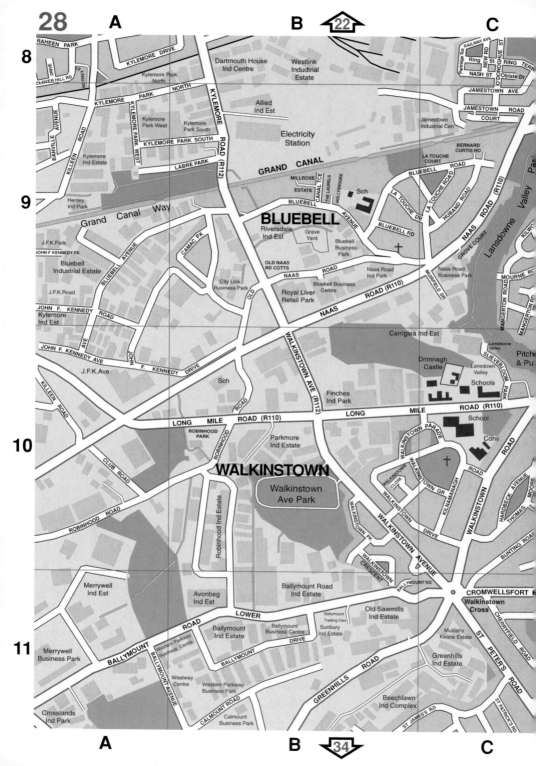

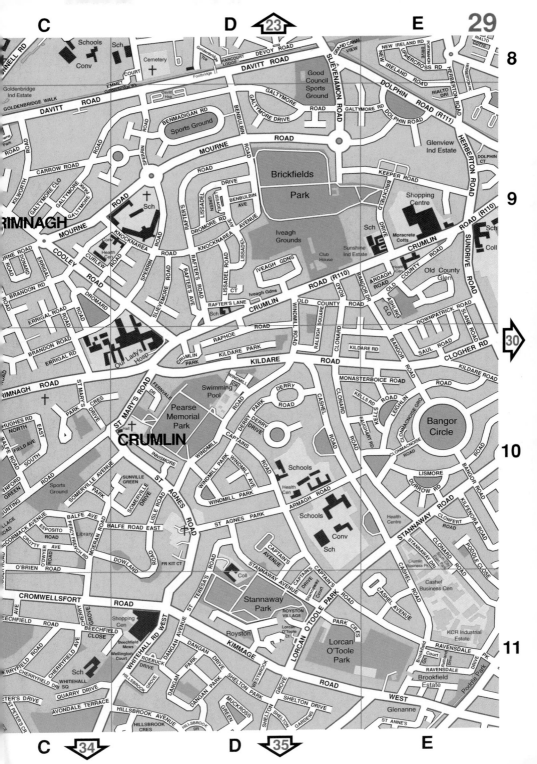

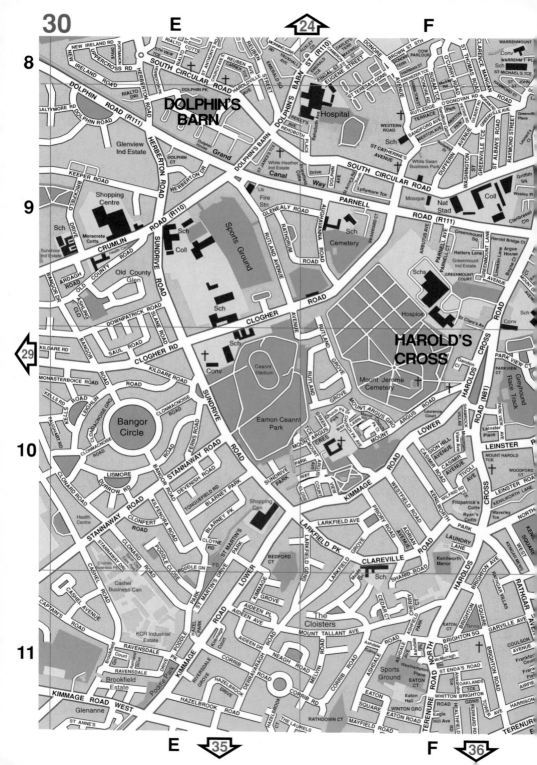

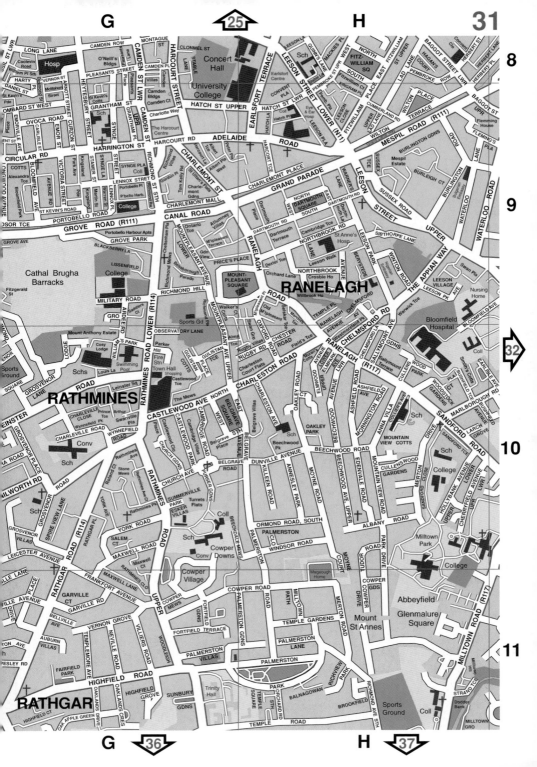

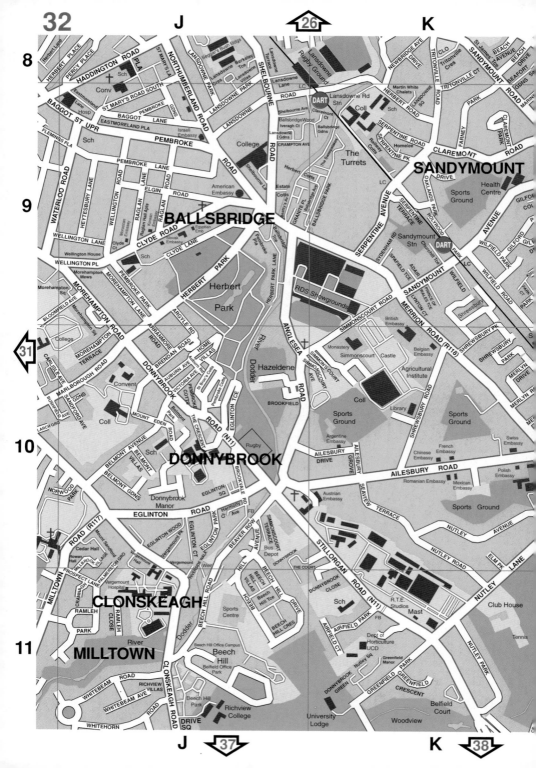

Sandymount
Strand

ORT AVENUE
VILLAS
Coll
Rehab
Inst
NGROVE
AVENUE
MARTELLO
VIEW
STRAND ROAD (R131)
DURHAM RD
LEA ROAD
CRES.
SANDYMOUNT CASTLE PARK
HAMPSTEAL TCE.

GILFORD AVE.
GILFORD
GILFORD ROAD
BETHANY
HOUSE
Sch
Conv
GILFORD TCE.

NILLOWFIELD
MARTELLO WOOD
Sports
Ground
Club House
Nursing
Home
Martello
Tower

PARK
St John's
St John's
ST JOHN'S RD EAST
STRAND LA.
SEABURY
RICHELIEU PARK
AVENUE
ADELAIDE
MARTELLO MEWS
MEWS
STRAND ROAD (R131)
MERRION STRAND
PARADE
DART
Sydney Pde Stn
ST ALBAN'S
WILLOW
MEWS
PARK
AILESBURY GDNS
AILESBURY MEWS

PARK
AVENUE
SYDNEY
MERRION CT.
BROOKLANDS
AILESBURY
Merrion
Village
Home
Nursing Home
FB
MERRION ROAD
+MERRION
MERRION GATES
Merrion
Strand

St Vincent's
Hosp
HERBERT AVE (R118)
ESTATE AVE.
Rehab
Centre
Level Crossing

Elm Park
Golf Course
St Mary's
Home
ROCK ROAD (R118)

BELLEVUE PK AVE
BELLEVUE AVENUE
DORNDEN PARK
BELLEVUE CT
BELLEVUE
PARK
BELLEVUE PK COPSE
DORNDEN
DORNDEN PARK
TRIMLESTON AVE.
WOODBINE ROAD
WOODBINE PARK
TRIMLESTON PK
TRIMLESTON PK
ST HELEN'S RD
ST HELEN'S VILLAS
Bathing Place
DART Booterstown Station

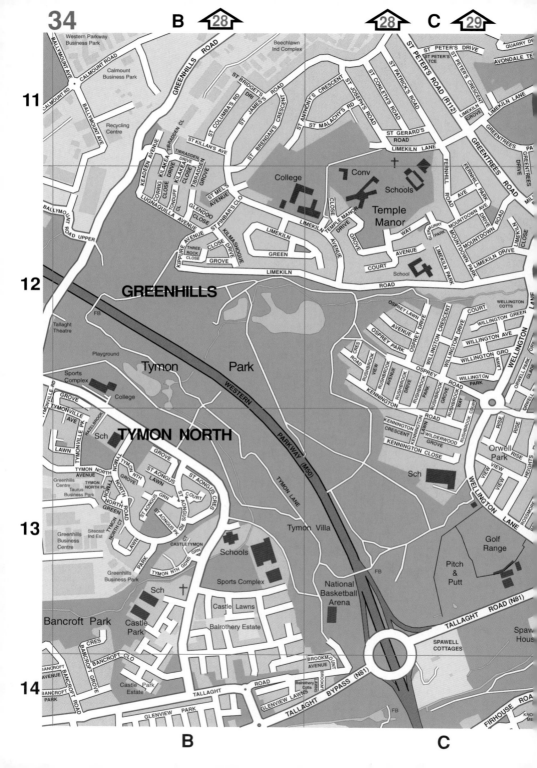

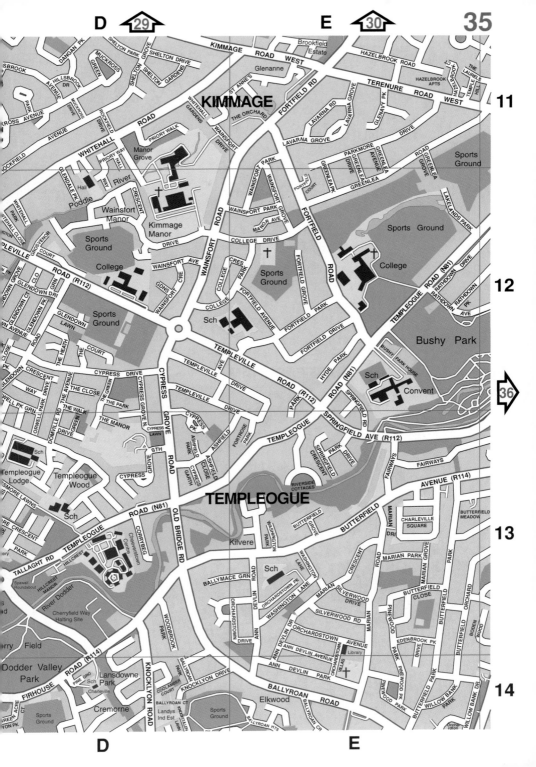

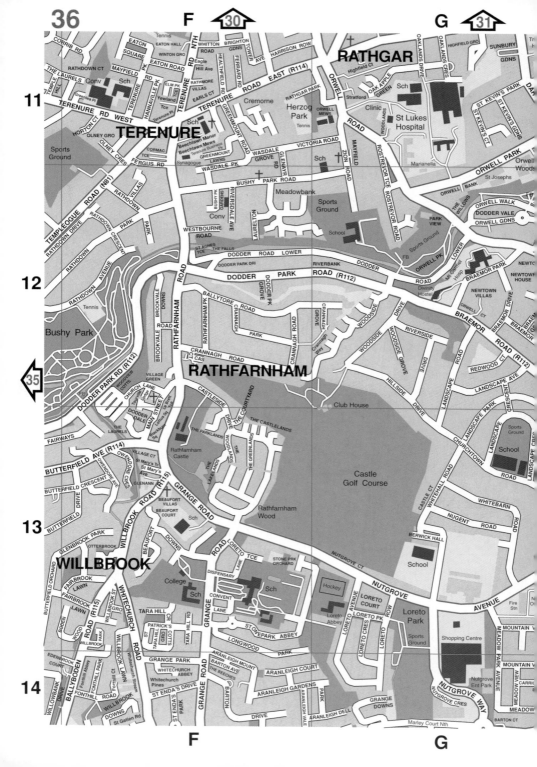

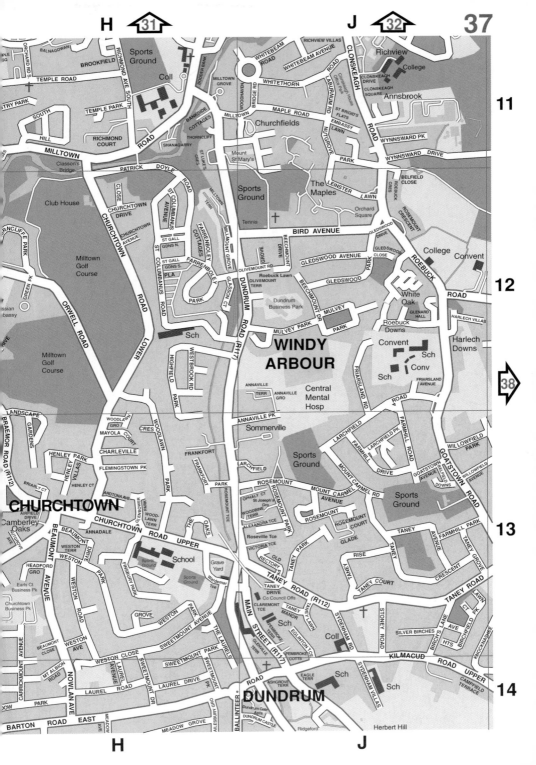

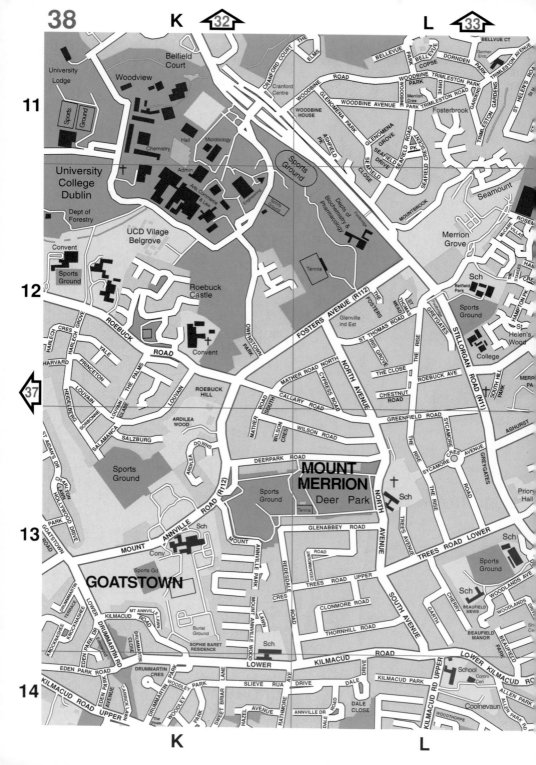

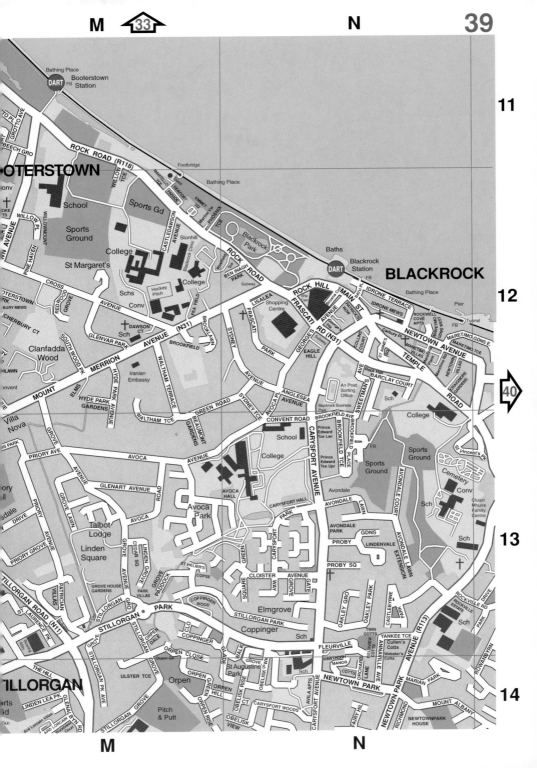

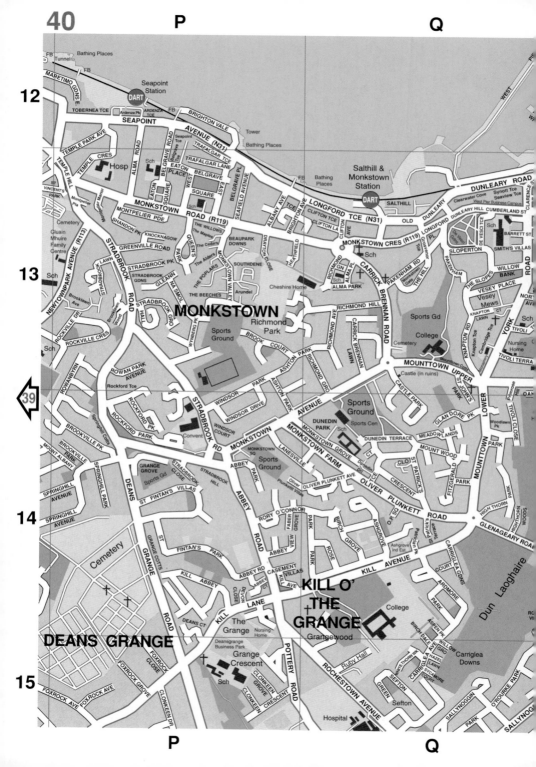

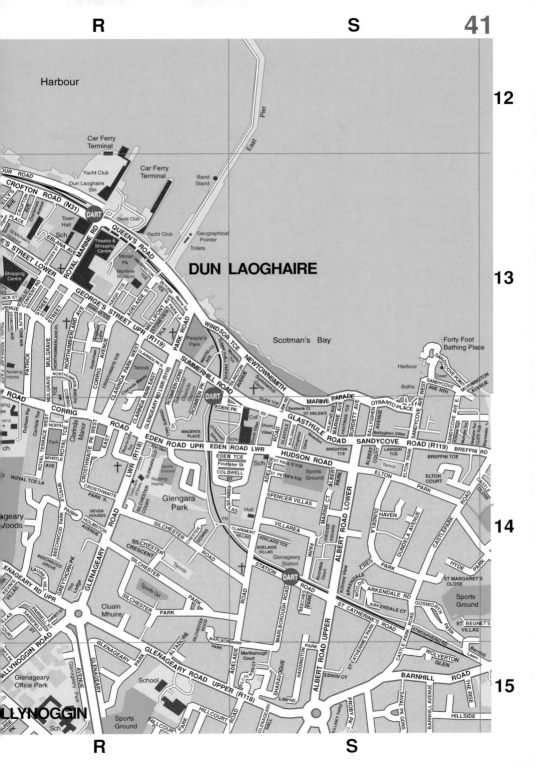

STREET INDEX

Due to insufficient space, some streets and/or their names have been omitted from the street map. Street names below which are prefixed by a * are not represented on the map, but they can be located by referring in the index to the name of the street which follows in brackets.

STREET INDEX

STREET INDEX

STREET INDEX

STREET INDEX

STREET INDEX

Dublin gets its name from the Gaelic, *dubh linn*, which means dark pool, a reference to the spot where the River Liffey meets the River Poddle. The first settlement near to this spot dates back more than 5,000 years.

Christianity arrived with Saint Patrick in 432 AD, and a golden age of Gaelic Christianity followed which produced such magnificent works of religious art as the Book of Kells which can still be seen today in Trinity College.

The native population remained largely undisturbed by further foreign visitors until the Vikings arrived early in the 9th century. Despite fierce resistance from the native Irish, the Norsemen consolidated their presence with victory in the Battle of Dublin in 919 and the town subsequently became an important trading post in the Viking empire.

The Vikings were finally overcome by the Gaelic clans at the Battle of Clontarf in 1014 but their influence is still marked today by place names such as Howth, from the Norse word *hovud* meaning headland, and Leixlip, from the Norse word *laxlep* meaning salmon leap.

The next invaders were Anglo Normans sent by King Henry II. Led by the Earl of Pembroke, who was better known as Strongbow, they landed in Wexford in 1169. Dublin was soon overwhelmed by the strength of their forces and the Normans quickly set about changing the urban landscape. Henry granted the town a charter in 1171 and established court there. The oldest surviving buildings in the city date from this period, including Christ Church and Saint Patrick's cathedrals, and parts of Dublin Castle. Due to the fact that wood was the main component of their construction, however, very little of the original buildings remain for us to see today.

English customs and the English language prevailed in and around the city, within an area which became known as the Pale, but Irish chieftains held sway elsewhere, giving rise to the phrase 'beyond the Pale'. By 1542, Henry VIII had proclaimed himself King of Ireland as well as England, and the Reformation came to Ireland. Dublin became Protestant, and grew in importance as royal authority spread to other parts of Ireland. By 1592 the College of the Holy and Undivided Trinity of Queen Elizabeth was founded on land confiscated from the Priory of All Hallows. Commonly known as Trinity College, this Protestant seat of learning has played an illustrious role in Dublin's history over the past 400 years.

With Charles I beheaded and the English monarchy abolished, Oliver Cromwell landed in Dublin with a large army in 1649, ushering in a particularly bloody and savage era in Irish history. After the restoration of the monarchy in 1660, Dublin began to take on much of the shape which we recognise today. St Stephen's Green and the Phoenix Park were laid out and many significant public buildings were erected including the Royal Hospital in Kilmainham, now the Museum of Modern Art.

By 1688, Catholic King James II had been deposed in favour of his daughter, Mary, who ruled jointly with her Protestant husband, William of Orange. Ireland was set to become a battlefield for a religious war involving most of Europe's major powers. In 1690 James lost the Battle of the Boyne to King William, and Catholics subsequently suffered under the Penal Laws, Gaelic culture was driven underground, and the seeds were sewn for the struggle for Irish autonomy from England.

The 18th century ushered in a golden age for Dublin when the city flourished both physically and culturally. Parliament House (now the Bank of Ireland), Custom House, the Mansion House, the Four Courts and Marsh's Library were all built during this period. Jonathan Swift, the author of *Gulliver's Travels*, returned to the city in 1713 to become Dean of St Patrick's Cathedral, and Handel came to Dublin and gave the first performance of his *Messiah* in 1742.

This golden age was short lived, however. The Act of Union of 1800 brought Ireland into a United Kingdom with Britain, and the seat of political power moved from Dublin to Westminster. The city's aristocracy followed and Dublin lost much of its social and cultural sparkle.

A century of political turmoil followed. Daniel O'Connell helped to achieve Catholic emancipation in 1829 and, as a Catholic middle class developed, Dublin started to become a distinctly Irish city. The city managed to escape the worst effects of the potato famine which decimated much of Ireland in the late 1840's, and it expanded rapidly as migrants flooded in from the surrounding countryside. The effect of the famine on the country as a whole was devastating, however. Out of a population of 8.5 million, approximately one million starved to death and a further 1.5 million emigrated, mainly to Britain and North America. The famine years served to heighten anti-British sentiment, and an abortive rebellion by the Irish Republican Brotherhood in 1868 led to calls for Irish Home Rule.

The case for Irish autonomy was taken up in the English parliament at Westminster by the Protestant leader, Charles Stewart Parnell. When Parnell died in 1891, he left a political vacuum which was eventually filled by two cultural movements, the Gaelic League which was set up to revive the Irish Language, and the Irish Literary Renaissance. William Butler Yeats played a pivotal role in restoring national pride with the foundation of the Abbey Theatre in 1904, giving prominence to playwrights such as Sean O'Casey and J. M. Synge. This cultural nationalism developed into political nationalism with the establishment of Sinn Féin (Ourselves Alone), a political movement which advocated a boycott of the English Parliament. With Britain engaged in the

O'Connell Bridge spanning the River Liffey

First World War, Sinn Féin organised the occupation of several strategic buildings around Dublin, and declared an Irish republic from its headquarters in the General Post Office on Easter Monday 1916.

The Easter Rising was quashed after six days of fighting with British forces, who numbered 20,000 troops, and 15 of the rebel leaders were later executed. A wave of public sympathy resulted, and Sinn Féin secured an overwhelming victory in the 1918 elections. A War of Independence between British and Irish republican armies soon followed and, after two years of fighting, General Michael Collins signed a treaty in 1921 which resulted in the creation of the Irish Free State, comprising 26 of Ireland's 32 counties. The other six counties became known as Northern Ireland and remained within the United Kingdom. Collins said at the time that he was signing his own death warrant and he was proved right the following year.

The treaty caused division between different factions within Sinn Féin and a bitter Civil War broke out which lasted for a year and saw the destruction of much of the city. Eamon de Valera won the battle for political control of the new state, and a period of political and cultural conservatism ensued which lasted until the late 1950's.

Ireland was declared a republic in 1949, but it was not until the 1960's that Dublin started to look outward. De Valera stepped down in 1959 to assume the figurehead role of Irish President, and a new *Taoiseach* (Prime Minister), Sean Lemass, assumed power and began the process of modernisation and industrialisation. Perhaps the most defining moment in Dublin's recent history, however, was Ireland's admission to the European Economic Community in 1973.

Over the past thirty years, Ireland has been transformed from a predominantly agricultural country into a vibrant industrial economy. Dublin today is a modern European capital which boasts a young and well educated population which has proved attractive to many foreign investors. Church and government are becoming increasingly disentangled as evidenced by the 1995 referendum result in favour of divorce, and liberalisation of laws in relation to homosexuality and abortion.

The government's initiative in setting up the International Financial Services Centre in the heart of the city has succeeded in attracting many of the world's leading investment banks, making Dublin an important offshore financial centre. Ireland is also at the cutting edge in electronics and information tech-

Irish Famine memorial on Custom House Quay

nology, ranking second only to the USA as an exporter of computer software, supplying around 40% of the European market. Economic progress during the 1990's was startling, and by the turn of the millennium the 'Celtic tiger' was enjoying an income per head which exceeded that of the UK for the first time in Irish history.

This process of modernisation has brought problems as well as benefits, however. Drug culture and organised crime have prospered alongside the rest of the economy despite the war waged against them by the police. Corruption in business and government has become a long running soap opera in the shape of the public tribunals set up to investigate some very shady dealings. After centuries of dispersing its citizens to the four corners of the earth, Ireland has become a magnet for economic migrants, resulting in a new air of multi-culturalism which has not been universally welcomed. Congestion has increased to the point where driving through Dublin

tends to take place at a pace somewhere between slow and stop.

The global downturn in the technology and banking sectors, together with the sharp falls in international travel following September 11 and war in Iraq, have left many Dubliners feeling that the party has ended in a hangover. High levels of begging on the street are an every day reminder that economic prosperity has failed to eradicate social inequality.

Thankfully, though, Dublin retains much of its Georgian charm and grandeur. For a city with a population of around one million people, it is compact and intimate, with many of its attractions within walking distance of one another. This factor, together with its rich literary tradition and reputation for youthful exuberance and a friendly welcome, makes it one of the world's favourite tourist destinations.

Whether you are living here or merely passing through, the sections which follow will try to help you make the best of all that Dublin has to offer.

AIR TRAVEL

Dublin Airport, which lies about 7 miles north of the city centre, is the international gateway for flights to many destinations across Europe and North America. Aer Lingus is Ireland's national airline, operating several domestic services out of Dublin in addition to its international routes. **Aer Rianta**, the airport managers, provide a comprehensive flight information service. Phone 814 1111 or visit their web site at www.dublin-airport.com

International and domestic arrivals and departures share the same terminal building - arrivals are upstairs and departures are downstairs. The airport handles more than 15 million passengers annually and can feel rather chaotic at times, despite recent costly improvements. Facilities include a foreign exchange counter in the arrivals area, a bank with extended opening hours, cash machine, post office and a very good tourist information office downstairs, as well as a much improved array of bars, restaurants, cafés and shops. The tourist information office is a good first stop for directions, information, and accommodation inquiries if you have not already booked.

Airlink, an express bus service, operates from outside the arrivals hall. Service number 747 stops in the city centre on O'Connell Street before going on to Busáras, the central bus station which is only a couple of minutes walk from Connolly Rail Station. Service 748 stops at Busáras, Tara Street Dart Station, Aston Quay, Wood Quay and Heuston Rail Station. Frequency of departures varies from ten to thirty minutes depending on the time of day. The first service is at 5.45am, the last at 11.20pm, the single fare is €5 and a return costs €7.50. Tickets can be bought from the CIE Information Desk in the arrivals hall and the journey into the city normally takes around half an hour, depending on traffic (allow an extra 15 minutes to Heuston Station). **Aircoach** offers an alternative service which leaves every 15 minutes and includes stops at many of the city's major hotels. Tickets cost €6 single, €10 return, and can be bought at the bus stop outside the terminal building.

Dublin Bus numbers 41 and 16A offer a cheaper alternative into the city centre but journey times are longer as these are normal suburban services.Similarly, Dublin Bus number 746 offers a cheap means of reaching areas south of the city such as Donnybrook, Stillorgan and Dun Laoghaire without having to stop off in the centre of town. Services depart from in front of the arrivals hall.

A cab from the taxi rank in front of the terminal building will take you into the city centre for around €20 (no extra charge for the wise-cracking which tends to be the hallmark of Dublin cabbies).

Avis, Budget, Eurodollar and Hertz all have car hire desks in the terminal building, and a number of other operators will deliver cars for collection at the airport. Renting a car can be an expensive exercise in Ireland, mainly due to the high cost of insurance, and it usually pays to shop around. Pre-booking through a travel agent will avoid the disappointment of not being able to get hold of a car, which can sometimes happen during the summer months. Given that life behind the steering wheel in Dublin is often a frustrating one, and that the city centre is a very walkable one, you might well wonder why you bothered to hire a car in the first place!

FERRY SERVICES

There are two ferry ports in Dublin and your point of arrival will usually depend on your choice of ferry company.
Dublin Port, served mainly by Irish Ferries, is situated just a couple of miles from the city centre in a run down area of town known as the North Wall. Dublin Bus number 53 will take you the short distance into town.

Dún Laoghaire Port, served by Stena Line, is about seven miles south of the city centre and it is served by the DART train as well as Dublin Bus numbers 7,46A and 746. The DART station is adjacent to the ferry terminal and the trains are fast and frequent. The terminal building has its own tourist information office which dispenses plenty of useful information and offers a booking service if you are in search of accommodation.

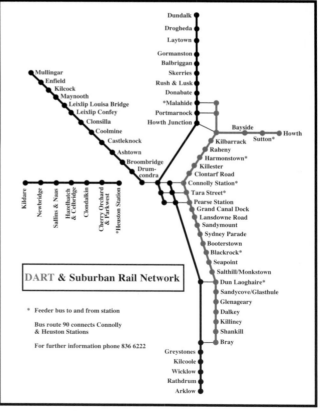

DART & Suburban Rail Network

* Feeder bus to and from station

Bus route 90 connects Connolly & Heuston Stations

For further information phone 836 6222

TRAINS

Irish rail services, including the **DART,** are operated by **Iarnród Éireann (Irish Rail)**, and their Travel Centre at 35 Lower Abbey Street is a good place to gather information and make bookings. Phone 836 6222 for information on all services or visit their web site at www.irishrail.ie

Inter City Trains

Rail journeys to Belfast, Sligo, Rosslare Harbour and Wexford start from **Connolly Station** (see page 25, grid reference H7) which is about ten minutes walk from O'Connell Bridge. Services to Westport, Galway, Limerick, Killarney, Tralee, Cork and Waterford leave from **Heuston Station** (see page 24, grid reference E7) which is a short bus or taxi ride to the west of the city centre. Bus service number 90 runs every ten minutes between Connolly and Heuston Station, stopping at Busáras, the central bus station, along the way.

The rail network is adequate, covering most major towns and cities, but you will probably have to rely on bus services if you want to reach smaller towns. If you are expecting bullet trains, forget it. Services have been upgraded in recent years, most notably the Dublin to Belfast line, but even inter city trains take about two hours to cover a distance of 100 miles.

Travelling by train tends to cost more than going by bus but there are discounts available for students with an ISIC card (International Student Identity Card), and for anybody under the age of 26 who invests in a European Youth Card (available from USIT at 19 Aston Quay). To take advantage of the discounts, however, it is necessary to stump up further for a TravelSave Stamp.

A selection of rail and/or bus passes is available if you intend exploring the country as a whole. For example, €105 will buy you an Irish Explorer rail pass which allows 5 days of travel within any 15 day period on all trains within the Republic of Ireland. Phone 836 6222 for further information.

Suburban Trains

Suburban services offer some very cheap travel. Trains leaving from Connolly Station head north as far as Dundalk, south as far as Arklow, and northwest as far as Mullingar. Services leaving from Heuston Station head west as far as Kildare (see route map opposite). Suburban trains use the same track as the DART but they make far fewer stops and therefore offer a good way of making day trips to places such as Malahide, Castletown House in the village of Celbridge, or Newgrange which is near Drogheda.

DART

The DART, or Dublin Area Rapid Transit, is a cheap but excellent electric rail service linking the city centre to various points along the coast of Dublin Bay, as far as Howth to the north, and Bray to the south (see the route map opposite). A more limited service goes further north to Malahide and further south to Greystones. The main city centre stations are Pearse and Tara Street Stations which lie just south of the River Liffey, and Connolly Station which is just north of the river (see page 25, grid H7). Services operate every 15 minutes (every 5minutes during the rush hour) from around 6.30am to 11.30pm Monday-Saturday, and less frequently from 9.30am to 11.30pm on Sunday.

Single fares start at around a euro but a range of travel passes offer useful savings for frequent users. For instance, a one day travel ticket which is valid for unlimited travel on the DART costs €6.50. A range of combined bus and rail tickets can also be purchased at very little additional cost (see page 64).

LUAS & Dublin Port Tunnel

If the city still looks like a construction site as you are reading this, it is probably due to two major infrastructure projects, the Dublin Port Tunnel and the LUAS tram project. The tunnel, which will run from the M1 motorway at Santry to Dublin Port, has been shrouded in controversy as costs have spiralled and it became apparent rather late in the day that it was not high enough to take some of the bigger trucks. When it finally opens in 2005, however, it will take 9,000 HGV's off the local road network. Congestion should ease further when the ambitious LUAS tram network is completed. The first lines from Tallaght to Connolly Station and from Sandyford to St Stephen's Green are due to start operating in 2004. The network will then be extended to Lucan, the Point Depot, and to the north of the city. Plans include underground Metro lines which will become part of an integrated urban transport system. Much more digging to come then.

BUS SERVICES

Dublin Buses

Until the future becomes reality, Dubliners will continue to rely primarily on **Bus Átha Cliath** (**Dublin Bus**) to get them from A to B using a comprehensive bus network which connects the city centre to all of the main suburbs of greater Dublin (see route maps on pages 64 & 65). Destinations and the service number are posted above the driver's window, with buses heading for the city centre displaying the Gaelic words, *An Lár*. Bus stops display the route numbers at the top and also provide additional route information on a revolving carousel. Travelling by bus is an inexact science, however, and timetables are therefore limited to the departure times from the terminus. Stops that display a "Set Down" sign are for buses which only let passengers off there, so don't wait around in the hope of getting on. The length of the queue at your stop is the best guide as to when the next bus is likely to arrive. Timetables can be obtained from Dublin Bus Head Office at 59 Upper O'Connell Street. For more detailed service information, telephone 873 4222 or visit their web site at www.dublinbus.ie

Buses start running from 6am Monday-Saturday, and 10am on Sundays. Services usually run every 10 to 20 minutes on popular routes although you may have to wait for an hour on some of the quieter routes. Last buses leave the city centre at 11.30pm (see Nitelink above and on page 64 for special late night services).

Tickets can be bought on the bus but you will need to have the exact fare ready in coins (notes are not accepted) as most routes operate an autofare system which means that drivers do not have access to cash for security reasons. Deposit your coins into the top of the fare box and, when the driver is satisfied, he will issue you a ticket. If you want to save time and money, however, a range of prepaid tickets can be purchased from Dublin Bus Head Office on Upper O'Connell Street, USIT on Aston Quay, the Tourist Office on Suffolk Street, and from many newsagents in the greater Dublin area. There are about 270 ticket agents and all have signs outside saying Dublin Bus Ticket Agent. Prepaid tickets are validated by a machine which you will find to your right as you board the bus. Some of these tickets allow combined access to bus, DART and suburban

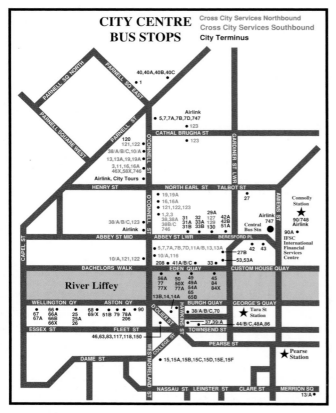

CITY CENTRE BUS STOPS

Cross City Services Northbound
Cross City Services Southbound
City Terminus

40,40A,40B,40C
• 1

Airlink
• 5,7,7A,7B,7D,747
• 123

120
121,122
38/A/B/C,10/A •
13,13A,19,19A •
3,11,16,16A •
46X,58X,746 •
Airlink, City Tours •

• 123

CATHAL BRUGHA ST

PARNELL ST

O'CONNELL ST

GARDINER ST LWR

HENRY ST
NORTH EARL ST   TALBOT ST
• 19,19A   27   Connolly
• 16,16A   Station
• 121,122,123
• 1,2,3   29A   Airlink
38,38A   31   32   127 42A   747
38/A/B/C,123 •   31A 33A 129 42B
Airlink •   38B/C 31B 33B 130 51A   Central
746   Bus Stn
ABBEY ST MID   ABBEY ST LWR   BERESFORD PL   90A •
                                             IFSC
• 5,7,7A,7B,7D,11A/B,13,13A   42 43   International
• 10/A,116   Financial
10/A,121,122 •   208 • 41A/B/C •   33 • —27B   Services
                                    —53,53A   Centre
BACHELORS WALK   EDEN QUAY   CUSTOM HOUSE QUAY

River Liffey
56A   50   49   45
77   50X   49A   84
77X   77A   54A   84X
13B,14,14A   65
              65B
WELLINGTON QY   ASTON QY   BURGH QUAY   GEORGE'S QUAY
• 66   • 68   • 90
67 66A   25   69/X 51B 79 78A   • 38/A/B/C,70   ★ Tara St
67A 66B   25A   206   Station
     66X   26   —37,39/A
ESSEX ST   FLEET ST   TOWNSEND ST   44/B/C,48A,86
46,63,83,117,118,150
                       PEARSE ST
DAME ST   ★ Pearse
WESTMORELAND ST   COLLEGE ST   Station
D'OLIER ST   HAWKINS ST
• 15,15A,15B,15C,15D,15E,15F

NASSAU ST   LEINSTER ST   CLARE ST   MERRION SQ
                                        13/A •

PARNELL SQ NORTH
PARNELL SQ EAST
PARNELL SQUARE WEST
CAPEL ST
AMIENS ST

rail services. A selection is outlined below but take note that pre-paid tickets are not valid for travel on Nitelink and City Tours, although Dublin Bus Rambler tickets can be used on Airlink services.

One Day Bus/Rail Ticket

Unlimited travel for one person: Travel by Dublin Bus costs €5; by Dart and suburban rail €6.50; by bus and DART costs €7.70.

One Day Family Bus/Rail Ticket

Unlimited travel for two adults and up to four children under the age of 16 : Travel by Dublin Bus costs €7.50; by Dart and suburban rail costs €11; by bus & DART and suburban rail costs €11.60.

Three Day Bus/Rail Ticket

Unlimited travel for one person: Travel by Dublin Bus costs €9.50; by bus, DART and suburban rail costs €15.

Seven Day Bus/Rail Ticket

Unlimited travel for one person: Travel by Dublin Bus costs €17.50; by bus, DART and suburban rail costs €26.

Monthly tickets are available if you are living in Dublin, and worthwhile price reductions are available to students with an ISIC Card and a TravelSave stamp which can be purchased from USIT at 19 Aston Quay.

Late Night Buses

Dublin Bus operate a late-night express bus service called **Nitelink** which will get you from the city centre to a wide range of suburban destinations, with a up to three pick-up points along the way. Nitelink buses display an 'N' after the route number and services operate every night of the week except for Sundays. Departure points are on Westmoreland Street, D'Olier St and College St. Most services depart at 12.30am and 2am Monday to Wednesday, and every twen-

ty minutes from 12.30am to 4.30am Thursday to Saturday. The fare for most routes is €4 but some longer distance routes cost €6. You can pay by cash, in coins only, on the bus, or purchase a pre-paid ticket from one of the yellow ticket buses located on the streets from where the services depart. Travel passes are not valid on Nitelink buses. For further information contact 873 4222.

National Bus Service

Bus Eireann (Irish Bus) is the national bus company, operating routes which cover the whole of Ireland. Fares, as a rule, are cheaper than going by train. All buses depart from Busáras, the central bus station, which is situated behind Custom House on Store Street (see page 25, grid H7). Tickets and information are available at Busáras or from the Bus Eireann desk in the Dublin Tourism Centre on Suffolk Street. Phone 836 6111 for more information or visit their web site at www.buseireann.ie

Bus Tours

Dublin Bus operate a range of daily tours all year round, but with increased frequency during the summer months. **The Dublin City Tour** (from an open-topped double decker, weather permitting!) lasts for an hour and fifteen minutes and leaves from outside Dublin Bus HQ on O'Connell Street. Stops include the Dublin Writers Museum, Trinity College, the National Gallery, St Stephen's Green, Dublin Tourism Centre, Dublin Castle, Christ Church Cathedral, St Patrick's Cathedral, Guinness Storehouse, the Museum of Modern Art, Dublin Zoo, the National Museum, and the Old Jameson Distillery. The tour runs at frequent intervals, normally every ten minutes, between 9.30am and 6.30pm. Tickets, which cost €12.50 per adult and €6 per child under 14, are valid all day and you can hop on and off the bus as the fancy takes you. **Irish City Tours** also operate a range of daily tours including their **Dublin Tour** which follows a similar route to that outlined above. Phone 872 9010 for more details.

If you want to be that little bit different and see Dublin both by land and water **Viking Splash Tours** will take you around the city on a 'duck', a World War II amphibious vehicle. The tour starts at Bull Alley Street, beside St Patrick's Cathedral, and winds its way around the city before taking to the waters of the Grand Canal! Departure times and prices vary according to the time of year but

DUBLIN BUS ROUTE NETWORK

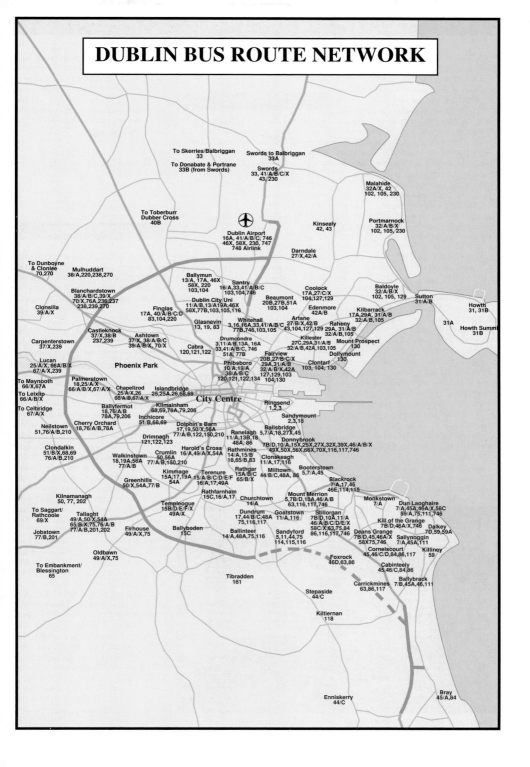

there are 10 tours a day during high season when the cost is €15.95 per adult and €8.95 for children under 13. The tour lasts an hour and 15 minutes. Phone 707 6000 for more information.

Dublin Bus's **Ghostbus Tour** can be good for a laugh as long as you are not spooked by tales of body-snatching and the like. The tour leaves Dublin Bus HQ on O'Connell St Monday to Friday at 8pm, and 7pm & 9.30pm Saturday to Sunday. The experience lasts 2 hours 15 minutes and costs €22 per adult.

If you would like to see beyond the city, Dublin Bus operate separate tours of the coastline to the north and south of Dublin. Both tours last about three hours and cost €20 per adult and €10 per child under 14. All tours start and finish outside the Dublin Bus HQ at 59 Upper O'Connell Street. Phone 873 4222 for more details.

Bus Eireann offer a wide range of sightseeing tours. Destinations include Glendalough & the Wicklow Mountains, Newgrange & the Boyne Valley, Kilkenny, Powerscourt, and the Mountains of Mourne. Phone 836 6111 for further details.

Irish City Tours offer a range of summertime tours both around Dublin and farther afield to places such as Newgrange, Malahide Castle, Powerscourt Gardens and Avoca. Phone 872 9010 for information or go to their reservations desk in the Dublin Tourism Centre in Suffolk Street. Alternatively, visit their web site at www.irishcity-tours.com

If you want to tour Ireland by bus, **CIE** offer a wide range of tours which include meals and overnight accommo-

dation. For more information, contact CIE Tours, 35 Lower Abbey Street. Phone 703 1888.

TAXIS

Dublin taxis can be hailed on the street or obtained at one of the many taxi ranks which can be found outside leading hotels, train and bus stations, and at strategic city centre locations such as O'Connell Street, College Green, and St Stephen's Green. The good news is that there are definitely more taxis on the road following recent controversial deregulation by Dublin Corporation. The bad news is that queues at taxi ranks can still seem a bit daunting at times, but bear in mind that it can feel like mission impossible getting hold of a cab on the street, especially late at night when the clubs are closing.

Fares are metered for journeys within 10 miles of the city centre, but there are numerous add-ons for additional passengers, luggage, and unsociable hours. Fares to outlying destinations should be agreed with the driver beforehand, but you should expect to pay about €1.50 per mile.

CAR HIRE

Renting a car in Ireland is usually an expensive exercise but, if you want to explore the country beyond Dublin, a car can be a necessity as the public transport system suffers from severe limitations. Cost will typically be somewhere between €250 and €400 per week depending on the car, the hire company, and the time of year. Despite the

cost, availability can sometimes be a problem during the summer months so it is advisable to book in advance. Avis, Budget, Hertz, Murrays Europcar and National Car Rentals all have car hire desks at Dublin airport, and a number of other operators will deliver cars for collection on your arrival.

Argus
59 Terenure Road East, Dublin 6. Tel 490 4444

Dan Dooley
Dublin Airport - Tel 844 5156

BICYCLE HIRE

Dublin is relatively flat and well suited to exploring by bike, although a good lock and a brave heart in traffic are both very important. Hiring a bike typically costs around €15 per day, or €50 per week.

Cycle-Ways
185 Parnell St, Dublin 1 - phone 873 4748

WALKING TOURS

Of the organised walking tours, the most informative are conducted by history graduates of Trinity College who will take you on a two hour **Historical Tour** of the city and share their considerable knowledge along the way. The tour takes in Trinity College, Old Parliament House, Temple Bar, City Hall, Dublin Castle, Wood Quay, Christ Church Cathedral and the Four Courts. Tours leave daily from the front gate at Trinity at 11am & 3pm from April to September, and at noon on Friday, Saturday and Sunday during the rest of the year. Cost is €10 per head. Phone 878 0227 for group bookings. A new series of tours covering subjects as diverse as architecture, a sexual history of Ireland, and the birth of the Irish state leave the gates at 12 noon during the summer months.

If you like to combine walking with drinking, the **Dublin Literary Pub Crawl** offers a very entertaining tour of some southside pubs associated with Dublin's legion of thirsty writers. The tour starts upstairs at the Duke on Duke Street. Phone 670 5602 for information. **The Musical Pub Crawl**, on the other hand, aims to enhance your knowledge of Irish music, starting off upstairs at Oliver St John Gogarty's in Temple Bar. Phone 478 0193. See page 82 for more detail.

Tour the streets *and* the waterways of Dublin with Viking Splash

Some would argue that it's due to the free advertising that Ireland used to get when it kept winning the Eurovision Song Contest, but finding a bed when visiting Dublin can be difficult at times, especially at weekends and at any time during the height of the tourist season. For a capital city, Dublin is not over endowed with hotels and although more are opening all the time, supply has not managed to keep up with demand in recent years. The golden rule, therefore, is to book your accommodation, either directly or through an agent, before you arrive. A couple of weeks in advance should be enough notice during the quieter times of year, but a month or two might be required if you want to stay in one of the more popular hotels during the summer months.

If you have acted on impulse, however, and find yourself in Dublin with no accommodation booked, reservations can be made at one of the following tourist information centres: Dublin Airport, Dun Laoghaire Harbour, Suffolk Street, O'Connell Street, Baggot Street Bridge, and at the Square Towncentre in Tallaght. Telephone bookings can be made with a credit card by phoning freephone number 1800 668 668 66 from within Ireland (00 800 668 668 66 from UK). A deposit is payable at the time of reservation, but this amount is deducted when the final bill is being settled. Touch-screen booking services operate on a 24 hour basis at Dublin Airport, Dun Laoghaire Ferry Terminal, and outside Dublin Tourism Centre on Suffolk Street. Alternatively, reservations can be made by visiting Dublin Tourism's website at www.visitdublin.com.

A small cross section of accommodation is listed below. In an effort to keep things simple, the accommodation has been categorised as 'expensive', 'moderate' or 'budget'. Specific prices are not given as rates often vary according to the time of year and most of the more expensive establishments offer special deals, usually relating to weekend stays. laterooms.com can be a useful source of discounted hotel rooms, especially if you are booking less than a couple of weeks in advance. Some of the city's guest houses offer rather more interesting accommodation than many of the hotels and a couple of the better ones are included in the moderate category.

Family-run B&B's, or townhouses, form the bedrock of budget accommodation, costing around €40 per person

Accommodation Prices

Expensive: Expect to pay in the region of €120 to €200 per night per person sharing, including breakfast.

Moderate: Expect to pay between €50 and €100 per night per person sharing, including breakfast.

Budget: Most budget accommodation costs between €25 and €50 per night per person sharing.

Accommodation can be booked directly, or through the Tourist Board by phoning 1800 668 668 66 from Ireland or 00 800 668 668 66 from UK, or visit www.visitdublin.com

sharing, but most are located in the outer suburbs of the city. Premises approved by Bord Failte display a shamrock sign and bookings can be made directly or through the tourist information centres mentioned above. If you are looking for something cheap, but close to the city centre, hostels offer a realistic alternative now that they have shaken off their down-at-heel image. Some have conventional bedrooms but most offer clean and comfortable dorm-style rooms with shared bathrooms. They are inspected and registered by Bord Failte but are not graded. Price normally depends on how many are sharing, but rates are typically €15-€30 per person per night.

During the summer months, from about mid-June until mid-September, it is possible to book university accommodation at Trinity College and Mercer Court apartments (Royal College of Surgeon's), both of which are right in the heart of the city centre, at UCD to the south of the city centre, and at Dublin City University to the north. Self catering and bed & breakfast accommodation is available and prices start from around €40 per person per night for a single room.

All Dublin hotels are inspected by Bord Failte (the Irish Tourist Board), and each is given a star rating, from one to five stars, to reflect the standard of the accommodation and the facilities available. Guest houses, which tend to be less expensive than hotels, are rated on a similar system, from one to four stars. The appropriate star rating is listed below after the name of each establishment. The hotels and guest houses selected tend to provide rooms with en suite bathroom facilities as standard.

For a more comprehensive list, Dublin Tourism publish an accommodation guide called where to Stay in Dublin which you can purchase from their information centres or via their web site at www.visitdublin.com.

EXPENSIVE

Burlington Hotel**** `31 H9`
Upper Leeson Street, Dublin 4
Phone 660 5222. 506 bedrooms
Dublin's largest hotel. An uninspiring exterior but inside is warm, comfortable and friendly, with a lobby which teems with life throughout the day and long into the night. Entry to the hotel nightclub, Annabel's, is free to guests.

Clarence Hotel `25 G7`
6-8 Wellington Quay, Temple Bar
Phone 670 9000. 50 bedrooms
Probably the trendiest hotel in town, largely due to the fact that it's owned by the rock band, U2. The hotel restaurant, the Tea Room is rated among the best in Dublin. The penthouse suite with its roof-top hot-tub overlooking the Liffey is a good place to impress the new woman or man in your life, or simply a good place to put some new life into the one you already have.

Jurys Ballsbridge Hotel***** `32 J9`
Pembroke Road, Dublin 4
Phone 660 5000. 303 bedrooms
Along with The Towers next door, this is the flagship of the Jurys group. Facilities include a swimming pool and gym.

Merrion Hotel***** `25 H8`
Upper Merrion Street, Dublin 2
Phone 603 0600. 143 bedrooms

Georgian grandeur at the Shelbourne

Situated across the road from the Irish Parliament, the Merrion started life as four Georgian townhouses. Careful restoration has ensured that the hotel retains much of the charm and elegance of the original buildings.

Shelbourne Hotel*** `25 H8`
27 St. Stephen's Green, Dublin 2
Phone 663 4500. 190 bedrooms
This is the grand old lady of Dublin hotels. Georgian elegance is the hallmark of the Shelbourne, although only the very finest, and most expensive, bedrooms get to enjoy the view over St Stephen's Green.

Westbury Hotel*** `25 G8`
off Grafton Street, Dublin 2
Phone 679 1122. 204 bedrooms
Located just off Grafton Street, the Westbury is one of Dublin's leading hotels and an ideal base from which to enjoy the city's shops and nightlife.

MODERATE

Bewley's Hotel* `32 K9`
Merrion Road, Dublin 4
Phone 668 1111 . 304 bedrooms
Situated close to the RDS in the fashionable suburb of Ballsbridge. Rooms and suites are offered at a fixed rate, with rooms available for around €100.

Comfort Inn* `25 G8`
95-98 Talbot street, Dublin 1
Phone 874 9202. 48 bedrooms
Large, stylish guesthouse, just off O'Connell St, and close to Connolly

Station.

Jurys Inn Christchurch* `25 G8`
Christchurch Place, Dublin 8
Phone 454 0000. 182 bedrooms
The distinguishing characteristic of a Jurys Inn is that guests pay a flat rate per room, rather than paying per person in the room. This has proved to be a popular and successful formula which Jurys have developed throughout Ireland and Great Britain. Each room can accommodate up to three adults, or two adults and two children. Jurys Inns tend to be large, modern, three star establishments with good facilities, and this one benefits from a pleasant location opposite Christ Church Cathedral, only a few minutes walk from Temple Bar. Expect to pay around €100 for a room, excluding breakfast. Jurys attract a lot of business, so try to book well in advance.

Jurys Inn Custom House* `25 H7`
Custom House Quay, Dublin 1
Phone 607 5000. 239 bedrooms
Overlooking the Liffey, next to the International Financial Services Centre, the format is the same as its sister hotel in Christchurch. (see above).

Fitzwilliam Guesthouse* `25 H8`
41 Upper Fitzwilliam Street, Dublin 2
Phone 662 5155. 12 bedrooms
Characterful guesthouse, situated in the heart of Georgian Dublin, only a few minutes walk from St Stephen's Green.

Stauntons On The Green* `25 H8`
83 St. Stephen's Green, Dublin 2
Phone 478 2300. 30 bedrooms
Elegant Georgian guest house overlooking St Stephen's Green. Own private garden and an enviable location which is handy for just about everything.

BUDGET

Avalon House `25 G8`
55 Aungier Street, Dublin 2
Phone 475 0001
Well run hostel accommodation for almost 300 guests in single, twin, four and multi-bedded rooms. Convenient location within easy walking distance of St Stephen's Green, Grafton Street and Temple Bar.

Dublin City University `7 H3`
Glasnevin, Dublin 9
Phone 700 5736. Approx 250 bedrooms
Single and double en suite bedrooms in

modern apartment blocks located about three miles to the north of the city centre. Rooms are either en suite or share a bathroom with one other. Price includes access to the campus facilities. Mid-June to mid-September.

Oliver St John Gogarty's `25 G7`
18-21 Anglesea Street, Temple Bar
Phone 671 1822
Modern hostel accommodation which caters for individuals and groups of up to ten people sharing. For the more flexible budget, Gogarty's also offer comfortable rooftop apartments with kitchen, TV and washing machine.

Kinlay House `25 G8`
2-12 Lord Edward Street, Dublin 8
Phone 679 6644. 33 bedrooms + 1 dorm
One of the largest and busiest hostels in the city, its location close to Temple Bar helps to maintain a lively atmosphere throughout the year. Accommodation is provided in twin, four, and six bedded rooms. Facilities include a cafe and a laundry, and prices include continental breakfast.

Mercer Court Campus `25 G8`
Lower Mercer Street, Dublin 2
Phone 478 0328. 100 bedrooms
Student accommodation serving the Royal College of Surgeons. Comfortable single and double, en suite rooms, right in the heart of town. Mid-June to mid-September.

Trinity College `25 G7`
College Green, Dublin 2
Phone 608 1177. Approximately 1,000 bedrooms
Not as cheap an option as one might expect, but don't forget that the historic city centre location is factored into the price, and parking is free. Accommodation ranges from rather monastic single rooms which overlook the cobbles and cost around €50, to modern self catering apartments on the edge of campus. Mid-June to mid-September.

University College Dublin `38 K12`
Belfield, Dublin 4
Phone 269 7111. Approx 1200 bedrooms
Modern self-catering accommodation set in the landscaped grounds of Dublin's largest university which is located about four miles south of the city centre. Individual rooms and apartments. Mid-June to mid-September.

Abbey Theatre
See page 76.

Arthouse Multimedia Centre `25 G7`
Curved Street, Temple Bar
Phone 605 6800
Arthouse is one of the flagship projects in the cultural redevelopment of the Temple Bar district. One of its main functions is to train artists in the use of computer technology. Facilities include a multimedia production unit, exhibition space, a cyber café, and a library which maintains a computerised database of contemporary Irish artists which can be accessed via the internet at www.arthouse.ie *Opening Times: Mon-Fri 10am-5.30pm.*

Bank of Ireland
2 College Green, Dublin 2 `25 G7`
Phone 677 6801
One of Dublin's most impressive buildings, the Bank of Ireland began life as Parliament House in 1729 but, when the Act of Union was passed in 1800, the government of Ireland was transferred to London, and the building was later sold and converted into a bank. The main banking hall now occupies what was once the House of Commons chamber but the House of Lords chamber has survived in tact. Items of interest include the parliamentary mace, an impressive Waterford crystal chandelier dating from 1765, and two large 18th century tapestries depicting the Battle of the Boyne in 1690 and the Siege of Derry in 1689. The building can be visited free of charge from Monday to Friday during banking hours, and there are guided tours of the House of Lords every Tuesday at 10.30am, 11.30am and 1.45pm.

Bank of Ireland Arts Centre `25 G7`
Foster Place, Dublin 2
Phone 671 1488
Originally the bank armoury, the centre is now home to 'A journey through 200 years of History' which chronicles the role played by the Bank of Ireland in the economic and social development of Ireland over the past two centuries. It also traces the history of the College Green building back to when it used to be the Irish Houses of Parliament. The centre also plays host to temporary exhibitions and is a regular venue for classical music recitals. *Opening Times: Tues-Fri 10am-4pm. Admission charge is €1.50 per adult.*

Beaches
The suburban rail system and the DART put quite a few sandy beaches within easy reach of the city centre. These include Dollymount, Malahide and Portmarnock to the north and Sandycove and Bray to the south.

Casino at Marino `18 K4`
Off Malahide Road, Dublin 3
Phone 833 1618
Not a casino, as we know it, but an architectural gem built in the 1760's as a pleasure house for the Earl of Charlemont in the grounds of Marino Estate. Marino House, however, was demolished in 1920 and much of the estate was sold off for development. Fortunately, the Casino, which actually means "small house", survives as a glorious folly. Tours of the building are conducted daily from 10am-6pm between June and September; 10am-5pm daily during May & October; Feb/March/Apr/Nov/Dec, Sun & Thurs 12noon-4pm. Admission charge is €2.75 per person.

Central Library
See page 74.

Chester Beatty Library
See page 74.

Chimney Viewing Tower `24 F7`
Smithfield Village, Dublin 7
Phone 817 3800
Panoramic views of Dublin available from a glass enclosed observation platform perched on top of the old Jameson distillery chimney. A glass walled lift takes you 220 feet above ground. *Opening Times: Mon-Sat 10am-5.30pm, Sun 11am-5.30pm. Admission charge €5 per adult.*

Christ Church Cathedral `25 G8`
Christchurch Place, Dublin 8
Phone 677 8099
The Cathedral of the Holy Trinity, or Christ Church as it is commonly known, is one of two Church of Ireland cathedrals in Dublin and the city's oldest building with sections dating back to 1172. The cathedral was founded by Sitric, the Norse King of Dublin, in 1030 but it was the Normans, led by Strongbow, who rebuilt the original wooden structure in stone. Much of the building collapsed due to subsidence in 1562 and most of what is seen above ground today is the result of major restoration work carried out during the 19th century. The vast crypt, which dates back to the Norman period, houses the Treasures of Christ Church exhibition. Choral Evensong takes place at 6pm on Wednesdays and Thursdays, 5pm on Saturdays (except July & August), and 3.30pm on Sundays. *Opening Times: Mon-Sun 10am-5pm. A donation of €3 per adult is requested. Entry to the treasury in the crypt is €3.*

City Hall `25 G8`
Dame Street, Dublin 2
Phone 672 2204
Completed in 1779 as the Royal Exchange, the building became the centre of municipal government in 1852. The City Hall's most striking feature is its interior rotunda with a central mosaic depicting the city's coat of arms, and a series of frescos depicting the heraldic arms of the four Irish provinces and var-

Trinity College - a tranquil oasis right in the heart of the city

Custom House reflected in the waters of the River Liffey

ious aspects of Dublin. A new exhibition entitled 'The Story of the Capital' traces the history of the city over the past 1,000 years. Admission is €4 per adult. Tours of the city hall are also available. *Opening Times: Mon-Sat 10am-5.15pm, Sun 2pm-5pm.*

Custom House `25 H7`
Custom House Quay, Dublin 1
Phone 888 2538
One of Dublin's finest Georgian buildings, Custom House has been a familiar part of the city skyline since it was completed in 1791. Designed by James Gandon, who was also responsible for the Four Courts, the building's classical facade is built from Portland stone and is best viewed from across the river. The rooftop statues of Neptune, Mercury, Plenty and Industry represent various aspects of transport and trade, and the statue on top of the central copper dome represents Hope. Although the building was ravaged by fire during the War of Independence in 1921, it was later restored. A visitor centre is located in and around the dome area of the building. Admission is €1 per adult. *Opening Times: mid March-Nov Mon-Fri 10am-12.30pm, Sat-Sun 2pm-5pm; Dec- mid March Wed-Fri 10am-12.30pm, Sun 2pm-5pm*

Dalkey Castle & Heritage Centre
Castle Street, Dalkey, Co. Dublin
Phone 285 8366
Restored 15th century castle housing a heritage centre which outlines the history of Dalkey, the surrounding area, and its many literary associations (chapter

two of Joyce's *Ulysses* was set in Dalkey), as well as providing exhibition space for Irish art and crafts. *Opening Times: Apr-Dec, Mon-Fri 9.30am-5pm, Sat & Sun 11am-5pm; Nov-Mar, Sat & Sun 11am-5pm. Admission charge is €7 per adult.*

Dublin Castle `25 G7`
Dame Street, Dublin 2
Phone 677 7129
Large parts of Dublin Castle have been rebuilt over the centuries and the building today is more palatial in style than one might expect. The original castle was built on the orders of King John in 1204 on the site of an earlier Viking fortification, remnants of which have been preserved and are on view at the 'Undercroft'. Dublin Castle was at the heart of British military and administrative rule in Ireland for 700 years and it was used during that time as a military fortress, a prison, record office, courts of law and residence of the British viceroys of Ireland. The fact that the statue of Justice above the main gate stands with her back turned towards the city was seen by Dubliners as an apt symbol of British rule. Presidents of Ireland are now inaugurated in the castle and its facilities are used to host European Union conferences and summits. The castle's State Apartments, Undercroft and Chapel Royal are open to visitors. *Opening Times: Mon-Fri 10am-5pm, Sat-Sun 2pm-5pm. Admission charge is €4.50 per adult.*

Dublin Civic Museum
See page 74.

Dublin Tourism Centre `25 G7`
Suffolk Street, Dublin 2
www.visitdublin.com
Phone 1850 230 330 from Ireland
Phone 0800 0397 000 from UK
Impressive premises housed in the former church of St Andrew. Services include tourist information and accommodation reservations for the whole of Ireland, a bookstore, gift shop, café, bureau de change, internet access, and booking facilities for theatres, bus & rail tours, and car rental. Other Information Centres can be found on Baggot Street Bridge, O'Connell Street, at Dublin Airport, Dun Laoghaire Harbour and at The Square in Tallaght.

Dublin Writers Museum
See page 74.

Dublin Zoo `15 D6`
Phoenix Park, Dublin 8. Ph 474 8900
The Zoo was founded in 1830 making it the third oldest in the world. It is situated in the Phoenix Park, within easy reach of the main entrance on Parkgate Street. The Zoo places a heavy emphasis on the breeding of endangered species, but there is plenty to see, including a daily feeding programme for gorillas, polar bears, reptiles, sea-lions and elephants. Areas include the 'World of Cats', the 'World of Primates', the 'Fringes of the Arctic', and a new 30 acre extension to the Zoo called the 'African Plains', with rhinos, hippos and giraffes among the residents. Ireland's number one visitor attraction. *Opening Times: Mon-Sat 9.30am-6pm (until dusk during winter); Sun 10.30am-6pm. Admission is €11 per adult, €7 per child, free for kids under 3.*

Dublinia `25 G8`
St Michael's Hill, Christchurch,
Dublin 8.
Phone 679 4611
Housed in the old Synod Hall beside Christ Church Cathedral, Dublinia tells the story of medieval Dublin from the arrival of Strongbow and the Anglo-Normans in 1170 to the dissolution of the monasteries by Henry VIII in 1540. Various displays, a scale model of the medieval city and a collection of artefacts from the Wood Quay site all help to bring this period of history to life. *Opening Times: April-Sept, Mon-Sun 10am-5pm; Oct-March, Mon-Sat 11am-4pm, Sunday 10.00am-4.30pm. Admission is €5.75 per adult.*

Four Courts `24 F7`
Inns Quay, Dublin 7
Home to the Irish law courts since 1796,

the Four Courts building has much in common with Custom House. Both were designed by James Gandon and both required major restoration following fire damage suffered during the turbulence of 1921 and 1922. The public is admitted only when the courts are in session.

Fry Model Railway Museum
See page 74.

GAA Museum
See page 74.

Gallery of Photography
See page 74.

General Post Office `25 G7`
O'Connell Street, Dublin 1
Phone 705 7000
The General Post Office was built in 1815 and is best known for its role as rebel headquarters during the 1916 Easter Rising. All but destroyed in the ensuing battle, it re-opened in 1929 and continues in public use today.

Grafton Street `25 G8`
Grafton Street is Dublin's premier shopping street and, as such, it is described on page 80. Even if you are allergic to shopping, however, it is still worth taking a leisurely stroll along this pedestrianised thoroughfare which also acts as an open air venue for some amusing street theatre, many talented buskers, and an array of other colourful characters.

Guinness Storehouse `24 F7`
St James's Gate, Dublin 8
Phone 408 4800
All you ever wanted to know about the 250 year history of the 'black stuff', from the brewing process through to the iconic advertising and merchandising of the product. Exhibition space covers seven floors of an impressive new visitor centre, and the tour finishes with a complimentary pint and panoramic views of the city from the Gravity Bar, which occupies the top floor of the building. Admission €13.50 per adult. *Opening Times: Mon-Sun 9.30am-5pm*

Halfpenny Bridge `25 G7`
Bachelor's Walk
The Ha'penny Bridge is a cast-iron footbridge which spans the Liffey, providing a convenient gateway to Temple Bar if you are crossing from the north side of the river. Built in 1816, the halfpenny toll no longer applies today!

Heraldic Museum
See page 74.

Hugh Lane Gallery of Modern Art
See page 74.

Irish Film Centre
See page 74.

Irish Jewish Museum
See page 74.

Irish Museum of Modern Art
See page 74.

James Joyce Centre
See page 74.

James Joyce Museum
See page 75.

Kilmainham Gaol `23 D8`
Inchicore Road, Kilmainham, D8
Phone 453 5984
The jail opened in 1796 but has not held any prisoners since 1924. Today it is a museum to the countless Irish patriots who were imprisoned here from 1798 until the release of the last inmate, Eamon de Valera, who went on to become Prime Minister, then President of Ireland. The darkest episode in the gaol's history was the execution of Patrick Pearse, James Connolly and 14 other leaders of the 1916 Easter Rising. A guided tour of the jail includes an audio-visual presentation and various exhibits relating to the struggle for Irish independence. The gaol has been used many times as a film location, including an appearance in the *Italian Job*. *Opening Times: Apr-Sept, Mon-Sun 9.30am-5pm; Oct-Mar, Mon-Sat 9.30am-4pm, Sun 10am-5pm. Admission is €5 per adult.*

Leinster House `25 H8`
Kildare Street, Dublin 2
Leinster House is the seat of Irish government; home to Dáil Eireann (House of Representatives) which comprises 166 elected TD's, and Seanad Eireann (Senate) to which 60 senators are appointed. Erected in 1745, the building is only open to the public when parliament is not sitting.

Malahide Castle `25 G7`
Malahide, County Dublin
Phone 846 2184
This charming castle has been both a fortress and the family home of the Talbots for nearly 800 years, right up until the last Lord Talbot died in 1973. The architecture reflects many different styles, and the interior is enhanced by an impressive collection of period furniture and an historic series of Irish portraits,

The spiritual Chester Beatty Library

most of which are on loan from the National Gallery. The castle stands in 250 acres of park land which is also open to the public. *Opening Times: Apr-Oct, Mon-Sat 10am-5pm, Sun 11am-6pm; Nov-Mar, Mon-Sat 10am-5pm, Sun 11am-5pm. Admission charge is €6 per adult.*

Mansion House `25 H8`
Dawson Street, Dublin 2
The Mansion House has been the official residence of the Lord Mayor of Dublin since 1715. The first Irish Parliament met here in 1919 to adopt Ireland's Declaration of Independence. The house is not open to the public.

Marsh's Library
See page 75.

Merrion Square `25 H8`
The best preserved Georgian square in Dublin and, as the wall plaques indicate, home to many historic figures including Daniel O'Connell and W B Yeats. The public gardens in the centre of the square are a hidden gem and well worth a stroll on a sunny afternoon.

Millennium Spire `25 G7`
One of Dublin's newest landmarks, known locally as 'the spike', the stainless steel spire forms a focal point for the redevelopment of O'Connell St. At 120 metres in height, it stands in a place formerly occupied by Lord Nelson until he was blown off his column by the IRA back in the 1960's.

National Botanic Gardens `16 F4`
Glasnevin, Dublin 9

The National Gallery of Ireland - one of the leading state galleries in Europe

in an act of contrition for tearing down most of the rest of the street to build an ugly 1960's office block. *Opening Times: Tues-Sat 10am-5pm, Sun 2pm-5pm. Admission charge is €3.15 per adult.*

Old Jameson Distillery   `24 F7`
Bow Street, Smithfield Village, Dublin 7
Phone 807 2355
The Old Jameson Distillery guides you through the ancient craft of whiskey making with the help of an audio-visual presentation, a museum and, of course, the Jameson bar where you can sample a drop or two of the 'water of life'. *Opening Times: Mon-Sun 9.30am-6pm (last tour 5.30pm). Admission charge is €7 per adult.*

The Oscar Wilde House   `25 H8`
1 Merrion Square, Dublin 2
Phone 662 0281
A fine example of Georgian architecture. The Wilde family took up residence in 1855, and Oscar lived here until 1876. Following recent major restoration, the ground and first floors are open for guided tours on Monday, Wednesday and Thursday, 10.15am & 11.15am. Admission is €2.54 per person.

Phoenix Park   `23 D7`
The Phoenix Park is the largest city park in Europe, covering 1760 acres and surrounded by a wall which is 8 miles long. The park is predominantly open grassland, grazed by a herd of deer, but it has a few notable residents including the Irish President who lives at Aras an Uachtaráin, and the US Ambassador. The main visitor attraction is Dublin Zoo (see page 70), but another place of interest is the Phoenix Park Visitor Centre which is in the grounds of the old Papal Nunciature, near to the Phoenix monument (admission €2.75 per adult, use Ashtown Gate). For something a little bit different, catch a game of polo in the park from May to September. The main entrance to the park is on Parkgate Street.

RHA Gallery
See page 75.

St Mary's Pro Cathedral   `25 G7`
Marlborough Street, Dublin 1
Phone 874 5441
Despite the predominance of Catholicism, Dublin has not had a Catholic cathedral since the Reformation, and so worshippers have had to rely on 'the pro' since 1825. Plans to build a grander cathedral on Merrion

Phone 857 0909
The Gardens were founded by the Royal Dublin Society in 1795 and contain some 20,000 species of trees, plants and shrubs, many housed within Victorian curvilinear glasshouses. *Opening Times: March-Oct, Mon-Sat 9am-6pm, Sun 11am-6pm; Nov-Feb, Mon-Sat 10am-4.30pm, Sun 11am-4.30pm. Admission is free.*

National Gallery of Ireland
See page 75.

National Library of Ireland
See page 75.

National Museum of Archaeology & History
See page 75.

National Museum of Decorative Arts & History
See page 75.

National Museum of Natural History
See page 75.

National Photographic Archive   `25 G7`
Meeting House Square, Temple Bar, Dublin2. Phone 603 0200
A new, purpose-built offshoot of the National Library, housing 300,000 photographs, as well as exhibition space and a reading room. *Opening Times: Mon-Fri 10am-5pm. Admission is free.*

National Print Museum
See page 75.

National Transport Museum
See page 75.

National Wax Museum
See page 75.

Newbridge House
Donabate, Co. Dublin
Phone 843 6534
Magnificent manor, built for the Archbishop of Dublin in 1740. The house stands in 350 acres of park land and boasts one of the finest Georgian interiors in Ireland. There is much of interest outside as well as in, including a dairy, a blacksmith's forge and a 29 acre traditional farm, complete with farmyard animals. *Opening Times: April-Sept, Tues-Sat 10am-5pm, Sun 2pm-6pm; Oct-March, Sat & Sun 2pm-5pm. Admission charge is €6 per adult.*

Newman House   `25 H8`
85-86 St Stephen's Green
Phone 716 7422
Cardinal Newman founded a Catholic University here in the mid-19th century and former scholars include the poet Gerard Manley Hopkins and James Joyce. The building has some of the finest Georgian interiors to be seen anywhere in Dublin. *Opening Times: June-Aug, Tues-Fri, tours at 12noon, 2pm, 3pm and 4pm Admission cost is €4 per adult.*

Number Twenty Nine   `25 H8`
29 Fitzwilliam Street Lower, Dublin 2
Phone 702 6165
Fitzwilliam Street epitomises Georgian Dublin and the idea behind number 29 is to convey what it was like (from the inside) to live as a middle class Dublin family in the early 1800's. The house has been preserved by the Electricity Board

Square were thankfully abandoned even though the Church acquired the land back in the 1920's.

St Michan's Church `24 F7`
Church Street, Dublin 7
Phone 878 2615
The church houses an organ which is thought to have been played by Handel, but the main attraction is the mummified bodies which can be viewed in the crypt! Guided tours, Mon-Sat, €3.50 per adult.

St Patrick's Cathedral `25 G8`
Patrick's Close, Dublin 8
Phone 475 4817
Like Christ Church, St Patrick's is a Church of Ireland cathedral with an ancient and chequered history. The current building dates back to 1191 but a church has stood on this site since 450 A.D., marking the fact that Saint Patrick used a well within the cathedral grounds to baptise converts into the Christian faith. The cathedral was ravaged by fires and storms during the 14th century and its appearance today owes much to 19th century restoration work paid for by the Guinness family. Jonathan Swift, author of *Gulliver's Travels*, was Dean of St Patrick's from 1713 to 1747, and he is buried within its walls. The cathedral's choir school was established in 1432 and the choir took part in the first performance of Handel's *Messiah* back in 1742. *Opening Times: Mon-Fri 9am-6pm, Sat 9am-5pm, Sun 10am-6pm. Admission charge is €4 per adult.*

St Stephen's Green `25 H8`
As soon as they glimpse the summer sun, many Dubliners make straight for the natural delights of St Stephen's Green. This urban oasis was originally a piece of common land used for public hangings among other things, but by 1880, it had become a public garden thanks to the benevolence of Lord Ardilaun, a member of the Guinness family.

Shaw's Birthplace `31 G9`
33 Synge St, Dublin 8
Phone 475 0854
Life for George Bernard Shaw, playwright and Nobel Prize winner, began in this Victorian terrace, and the interior has been restored to reflect life at that time. *Opening Times: May-Sept, Mon-Sat 10am-5pm, Sun 2am-6pm. Admission charge is €6 per adult.*

Temple Bar `25 G7`
The Temple Bar area is sandwiched between Dame Street and the river, with Westmoreland Street to the east and Fishamble Street to the west acting as its other boundaries. This is one of the oldest areas of Dublin but it had been in decline for many years when plans were made in the 1980's to redevelop a large part of it as a bus station. Enter Irish Taoiseach (Prime Minister), Charles Haughey, who decided that Temple Bar should become the beneficiary of several major cultural projects. Like President Miterrand of France, Mr Haughey hoped that his lasting legacy would be to the Arts although, as things turned out, most Dubliners remember him for his ability to attract large financial gifts. Temple Bar, as it happens, is often described as Dublin's Left Bank, and this is probably a fair description. The area, which is characterised by its narrow cobbled streets, is now peppered with galleries, design studios, theatres, cinemas, cultural centres, alternative shops and many good pubs, clubs and restaurants. During the summer months, Meeting House Square is home to **Diversions Temple Bar,** a free outdoor festival of contemporary culture which includes live performances, film screenings and family events. **The Temple Bar Food Market** also sets up in Meeting House square, every Saturday 10am-5pm. On the downside, the success of the area has attracted a lot of stag and hen parties, and celebrations have been known to get out of hand occasionally. Many businesses have recently responded by banning stag groups from pubs and clubs in Temple Bar. For more information on what's on in the area visit www.templebar.ie

Trinity College & The Book of Kells
College Street, Dublin 2 `25 G7`
Phone 608 2320
Founded in 1592 by Queen Elizabeth I and built on land confiscated from the Priory of All Hallows, Trinity College is the oldest university in Ireland. Despite its city centre location, the 40 acre campus is a tranquil world containing an

Mr Joyce admires the Millennium Spire

impressive array of buildings dating from the 17th to the 20th century. The college has had an uneasy relationship with the Catholic Church, and it was not until the death of Archbishop McQuaid in 1970 that the Church lifted its boycott and proclaimed that it was no longer a mortal sin for a Catholic to attend Trinity. The college displays many treasures, the best known being the Book of Kells, a 9th century illustrated manuscript of the Gospels, often described as 'the most beautiful book in the world'. Other visitor attractions include The Dublin Experience, a 45 minute audiovisual show which tells the story of Dublin from Viking times to present day. There is free public access to the College and it is well worth a visit just to sample the rarefied atmosphere of its cobbled squares and college greens. The Old Library is open Mon-Sat 9.30am-5pm, Sun 12noon-4.30pm. The Dublin Experience is open daily, late May to early October, 10am-5pm. There is an admission charge of €7 per adult to see the Old Library which houses the Book of Kells, and €4.20 to view The Dublin Experience.

Whitefriar Street Carmelite Church
56 Aungier Street, Dublin 2 `25 G8`
Phone 475 8821
The church stands on the site of a Carmelite Priory which was founded in 1278, but the current building was not started until 1825. The church contains several interesting relics donated by Pope Gregory XVI in 1835, the best known being the remains of St Valentine.

Christ Church Cathedral

The list that follows is certainly not an exhaustive one - Dublin has an array of small galleries dotted around the city, especially in the Temple Bar district. The admission prices listed are based on one adult, but concessions are normally available for children and groups, and sometimes for students and the unemployed. For more detailed information, simply phone the appropriate number given below.

Central Library `25 G7`
Henry Street, Dublin 1
Phone 873 4333
The library, which occupies the upper floor of the ILAC Centre, is the hub of Dublin's public library system. Facilities include a useful reference section, a language centre and a video viewing room. *Opening Times: Mon-Thurs 10am-8pm; Fri-Sat 10am-5pm.*

Chester Beatty Library `25 G7`
Dublin Castle, Dame Street, Dublin 2
Phone 407 0750
European Museum of the Year 2002, and a must-see attraction. The library's new home, which overlooks Dubh Linn Garden, a tranquil oasis in the grounds of Dublin Castle, houses a collection of 22,000 items bequeathed to the nation by Sir Alfred Chester Beatty in 1968, including a treasure trove of Islamic manuscripts, Chinese, Japanese, Indian and other Oriental art. Biblical papyri, other early Christian manuscripts, Western prints and printed books complete one of the richest collections of its kind in the world. A spiritual place. *Opening Times: Mon-Fri 10am-5pm (closed Mondays Oct-Apr), Sat 11am-5pm, Sun 1pm-5pm. Admission is free.*

Dublin Civic Museum `25 G8`
58 South William Street, Dublin 2
Phone 679 4260
Dublin Civic Museum aims to improve our knowledge and understanding of Dublin, its history and its people. Exhibits range from a collection of objects from Viking Dublin to the head from a statue of Lord Nelson which used to stand in O'Connell Street until it was blown up by the IRA in1966! *Opening Times: Tues-Sat 10am-6pm, Sun 11am-2pm. Admission is free.*

Dublin Writers Museum `17 G9`
18 Parnell Square North, Dublin 1
Phone 872 2077
Housed in a beautifully restored 18th century Georgian mansion, the Writers Museum opened in 1991 to mark the great literary tradition which Dublin has cultivated over the past 300 years. On display are letters, first editions, portraits and other personal items belonging to a galaxy of Irish writers including Joyce, Shaw, Beckett, Wilde, Yeats, Swift, Sheridan, O'Casey and Behan. The museum hosts exhibitions and readings and has a special room devoted to children's literature. *Opening Times: Mon-Sat 10am-5pm, Sun 11am-5pm. Late opening until 6pm Mon-Fri during June, July & August. Admission charge is €6 per adult.*

Fry Model Railway Museum
Malahide Castle Demesne, Malahide
Phone 846 3779
Impressive model railway layout which recreates much of Ireland's transport system in miniature and is complemented by separate displays of hand crafted railway models and other memorabilia. An absolute must for train spotters! *Admission price is €6 per adult. Opening Times: April-Sept, Mon-Sat 10am-5pm, Sun 2pm-6pm.*

GAA Museum `17 H5`
Croke Park, Clonliffe Road, Dublin 3
Phone 855 8176
The museum charts the history of the Gaelic Athletic Association since it was founded in 1884. Displays include trophies and artefacts from the games of Gaelic Football and Hurling, with audio visual and touchscreen technology on hand to help recall famous games and players from past and present. Interactive technology allows you to test your sporting skills. See where the action actually takes place with a tour of the stadium, which is Europe's 4th largest arena. *Opening Times: Mon-Sat 9.30am-5pm, Sun 12noon-5pm. Admission charge is €5 per adult for the museum, €8.50 to include stadium tour.*

Gallery of Photography `25 G7`
Meeting House Square, Temple Bar
Phone 671 4654
Ireland's only gallery devoted exclusively to photography plays host to both Irish and international exhibitions, which are accompanied by talks and workshops. Services available include restoring and copying old photographs. *Opening Times: Tues-Sat 11am-6pm*

Heraldic Museum `25 H8`
2 Kildare Street, Dublin 2
Phone 603 0311
Coats of arms are the subject here and, for a fee, the Genealogical Office will dispense advice on how best to trace your ancestry. *Opening Times: Mon-Wed* 10am-8pm, Thurs & Fri 10am-4.30pm, Sat 10am-12.30pm. Admission is free.

Hugh Lane Gallery of Modern Art `17 G6`
Parnell Square North, Dublin 1
Phone 8741903
Situated in Charlemont House, a magnificent 18th century townhouse, the gallery is named after Hugh Lane, an Irish art lover who bequeathed many major works to the gallery after his death in the 1915 sinking of the Lusitania. French Impressionists are well represented with works by Manet, Monet, Degas and Renoir, and there is also a large collection of Irish art including paintings by J B Yeats and stained glass panels by Harry Clarke. A recent exciting acquisition is the studio of Francis Bacon and its entire contents, numbering 7,500 items. The studio has been faithfully reconstructed as a permanent exhibit at the gallery. Free concerts and lectures on Sundays. *Opening Times: Tues-Thurs 9.30am-6pm, Fri & Sat 9.30am-5pm, Sun 11am-5pm. Admission is free to the permanent collection, €7 to the Francis Bacon Studio.*

Irish Jewish Museum `31 G9`
3-4 Walworth Rd, Dublin 8
Phone 453 1797
The museum, which is housed in a former synagogue, chronicles the history of Jews in Ireland. *Opening Times: May-Sept, Tues/Thurs/Sun 11am-3.30pm; Oct-April, Sun 10.30am-2.30pm. Admission is free.*

Irish Museum of Modern Art `24 E8`
Royal Hospital, Military Road, Kilmainham, Dublin 8. Phone 612 9900
Modelled on *Les Invalides* in Paris, the Royal Hospital was built in 1684, not as a hospital, but as a home for retired soldiers and it remained so until early this century. One of the finest buildings in Ireland, it was restored in 1986 and opened as a museum in 1991. Its permanent collection, together with temporary exhibitions, provide a showcase for Irish and international art mainly from the second half of the 20th century. *Opening Times: Tues-Sat 10am-5.30pm, Sun 12noon-5.30pm. Admission is free.*

James Joyce Centre `17 G6`
35 Nth Great George's St, Dublin 1
Phone 878 8547
The James Joyce Centre is housed in a beautifully restored 18th century Georgian townhouse which, although associated with Joyce, was never actually his home. The centre promotes the life and work of Joyce with daily talks, con-

ducted tours of the house, and a walking tour through the Joyce country of north Dublin. Facilities include a coffee shop and bookshop, and visitors are welcome to use the Guinness Reference Library. *Opening Times: Mon-Sat 9.30am-5pm, Sun 12noon-5pm. Admission to the house is €4.50 per adult. Walking tour €9.*

James Joyce Museum
Joyce Tower, Sandycove
Phone 280 9265
The museum is housed in a Martello Tower where Joyce stayed for a week in 1904 as the guest of Oliver St John Gogarty who inspired Joyce to create the unsavoury character, Buck Mulligan. Much of the first chapter of *Ulysses* is actually set in the tower. Exhibits include letters, books, photographs and personal possessions of Joyce. *Opening Times: April-Oct, Mon-Sat 10am-5pm, Sun 2pm-6pm. Admission charge is €6 per adult.*

Marsh's Library `25 G8`
St Patrick's Close, Dublin 8
Phone 454 3511
Built in 1701 by Archbishop Narcissus Marsh, Marsh's Library is the oldest public library in Ireland. It was designed by Sir William Robinson who was also the architect for the Royal Hospital, Kilmainham. The library contains 25,000 books and manuscripts, most dating from the 16th to the 18th centuries. The interior is dominated by carved oak and includes three wired alcoves or 'cages' where scholars were once locked in while they studied rare volumes. *Opening Times: Mon/Wed-Fri 10am-1pm & 2pm-5pm; Sat 10.30am-1pm. Admission charge is €2.50 per adult, children free.*

National Gallery of Ireland `25 H8`
Merrion Square West, Dublin 2
Phone 661 5133
The National Gallery of Ireland first opened in 1864 but by the late 1980's it had fallen on hard times, so much so that one art-lover was able to remove a small French oil and post it back to the gallery in protest at the state of disrepair and lack of security. How times have changed. The Gallery has recently undergone major refurbishment which has seen the opening of a Yeats Museum, and a new 4,000 square metre extension, the Millennium Wing, which has its own entrance on Clare Street. It now ranks among the leading state galleries in Europe, attracting over one million visitors a year to view a collection which

includes work by Rembrandt, Titian, Goya, El Greco, Monet, Degas and Picasso. There are free guided tours at 3pm on Saturdays, and on Sundays at 2pm, 3pm and 4pm. *Opening Times: Mon-Sat 9.30am-5.30pm, Thurs 9.30am-8.30pm, Sun 2pm-5pm. Admission is free.*

National Library of Ireland `25 H8`
Kildare Street, Dublin 2
Phone 603 0200
With over half a million volumes and an historic collection of Irish newspapers, photographs, maps and prints, this is the country's leading library for Irish studies. You will need a reader's ticket, which can be obtained free of charge, to enjoy the Reading Room with its stately dome. *Opening Times: Mon-Wed 10am-9pm; Thurs-Fri 10am-5pm; Sat 10am-1pm.*

National Museum of Archaeology and History `25 H8`
Kildare Street, Dublin 2
Phone 677 7444
Opened in 1890, the National Museum contains a magnificent collection of Irish treasures and artefacts dating from the Stone Age to the 20th century. The Centrecourt houses 'Or - Ireland's Gold' exhibition featuring jewellry and metal work dating from the Bronze Age, 2,000 years ago. The Treasury displays the Ardagh Chalice, Tara Brooch, Cross of Cong and many other examples of outstanding medieval Celtic craftsmanship, accompanied by an audio-visual programme explaining their archaeological background. Other displays include Ancient Egypt, Viking Age Ireland and Medieval Ireland 1150-1550. *Opening Times: Tues-Sat 10am-5pm, Sun 2pm-5pm. Admission is free.*

National Museum of Decorative Arts and History `24 F7`
Collins Barracks, Benburb St, Dublin 7
Phone 677 7444
Housed in the oldest military barracks in Europe, this is a new museum space acquired by the National Museum to house its collection of decorative arts and artefacts relating to the economic, social, political and military history of the state. Displays include silver work, ceramics, glass, period furniture, weaponry, scientific instruments and textiles. *Opening Times: Tues-Sat 10am-5pm, Sun 2pm-5pm. Admission is free.*

National Museum of Natural History
Merrion Street, Dublin 2 `25 G8`
Phone 677 7444

The Natural History Museum has changed very little since Doctor Livingstone delivered the opening lecture in 1857. It houses a diverse collection of world wildlife, mainly of the stuffed variety. The ground floor is devoted largely to Irish mammals, birds, sea creatures and insects, and exhibits include the extinct giant Irish deer. The World collection is on the first floor and includes the skeletons of two humpback whales washed up on Irish shores, a giant panda and a pygmy hippopotamus. *Opening Times: Tues-Sat 10am-5pm, Sun 2pm-5pm. Admission is free.*

National Print Museum `26 J8`
Garrison Chapel, Beggars Bush Barracks, Dublin 4
Phone 660 3770
Museum dedicated to the preservation of the machinery and printing techniques employed before the advent of computers. *Opening Times: Mon-Fri 10am-5pm, Sat-Sun 12noon-5pm*

National Transport Museum
Howth Castle Demesne, Howth
Phone 847 5623
Museum run by a group of volunteers dedicated to the preservation of Ireland's transport heritage. Exhibits include old buses, trams, fire engines and military vehicles. *Opening Times: June-August, Mon-Sun 10am-5pm; Sept-May Sat & Sun 2pm-5pm. Admission charge is €3 per adult, €1.50 per child.*

National Wax Museum `17 G6`
Granby Row, Parnell Sq, Dublin 1
Phone 872 6340
The National Wax Museum serves up familiar offerings which include the Chamber of Horrors and the Hall of the Megastars where you can see the likes of Madonna, Elvis Presley, Michael Jackson and U2. Other features include the Children's World of Fairytale and Fantasy, and an array of famous, and not so famous, figures from Irish history. *Opening Times: Mon-Sat 10am-5.30pm, Sun 12noon-5.30pm. Admission charge is € per adult, €4 per child.*

RHA Gallery `25 H8`
15 Ely Place, Dublin 2
Phone 661 2558
The Royal Hibernian Gallery hosts major exhibitions of Irish and international art, in addition to its own collection of contemporary Irish art which is permanently on display. *Opening Times: Tues-Wed/Fri-Sat 11am-5pm, Thurs 1pm-8pm, sun 2pm-5pm. Admission is free.*

If you are planning an evening out at the theatre, cinema or a performance of live music or comedy, it's a good idea to pick up a free copy of *The Event Guide* which is published fortnightly and is available in many shops, cafés and venues around the city. Alternatively, you can invest €2.48 in a copy of *In Dublin* magazine which is similar in format to London's *Time Out*. It provides an excellent and comprehensive guide to what's on, including a series of current reviews. If you are on-line, try www.entertainment.ie for another source of up to date reviews and listings.

THEATRE

For a city steeped in literary tradition, it is only fitting that the Dublin theatre scene is a vibrant one. The Abbey is the most famous theatre in town, premiering the work of many Irish playwrights (see below). It occupies the mainstream along with the Gate and the Gaiety, but variety abounds, with theatres such as the Peacock, the Project, the New Theatre and the Focus staging many works of a more experimental nature. And with fresh writing talent such as Frank McGuinness and Martin McDonagh, Irish theatre goers are able to enjoy a good selection of contemporary drama as well as the catalogue of better known work from the past.

Dublin theatre is very accessible and need not be expensive. The dramatic societies of Trinity College and UCD may be amateur companies but their output is often of a high standard. Both societies perform two plays a week from October through to April, one at lunchtime and one in the evening. The prices are very cheap and Trinity Players Theatre is especially convenient to the city centre.

The highlight of the theatrical calendar is the Dublin Theatre Festival and its Fringe. The main festival runs for the first two weeks in October, while the fringe starts a week earlier and runs for three weeks. The theatre festival has been running for longer than the Edinburgh Festival and, like its Scottish counterpart, it manages to attract performers from the four corners of the globe. The festival programme is available from late August and booking begins three weeks before opening. The fringe festival focuses primarily on the lighter side of life and includes a wide variety of comedy, cabaret, dance and musical performances, staged at a multitude of smaller venues across the city, including many pubs. For more information,visit www.festival-ireland.ie.

Finally, when booking theatre tickets over the phone, it might be useful to refer to the seating plans published in the theatre section of the Golden Pages telephone directory.

Abbey Theatre `25 H7`
26 Lower Abbey Street, Dublin 1
Phone 878 7222
The Abbey and the Peacock, which share the same site, are the two theatres of the National Theatre Society which was founded in 1904 by W B Yeats, Lady Gregory and J M Synge. The original theatre was destroyed by fire in 1951 which explains the rather uninspiring 1960's replacement. One of the aims of the Society is to promote new Irish writing and, to this end, it has premiered the work of every leading Irish playwright this century including Sean O'Casey, J M Synge, Brian Friel and Frank McGuinness . The acting tradition of the Abbey is no less illustrious and the Society has produced many renowned actors such as Barry Fitzgerald, Ray McAnally and Cyril Cusack. The theatre has deservedly earned an international reputation for the quality of its productions which also include the work of playwrights from beyond Irish shores.

Andrew's Lane Theatre `25 G8`
9-13 St Andrew's Lane. Phone 679 5720

Bewley's Cafe Theatre `25 G8`
2nd floor, Bewley's, Grafton St. Phone 086 878 4001
Lunchtime drama - admission price includes soup and a sandwich.

Civic Theatre
Tallaght, Dublin 24. Phone 462 7477

Crypt Theatre `25 G7`
Dublin Castle, Dame St. Ph 671 3387

Focus Theatre `31 H9`
6 Pembroke Place. Phone 676 3071

Gaiety Theatre `25 G8`
South King Street. Phone 677 1717

Gate Theatre `17 G6`
1 Cavendish Row. Phone 874 4045

Helix `7 G3`
Collins Ave, Glasnevin, Dublin 9. Phone700 7000

Lambert Puppet Theatre `40 Q13`
5 Clifton La, Monkstown. Ph 280 0974

New Theatre `25 G7`
43 East Essex Street. Phone 670 3361

Olympia Theatre `25 G7`
72 Dame Street. Phone 1890 925130

Pavilion Theatre `41 R13`
Dun Laoghaire. Phone 231 2929

Peacock Theatre `25 G7`
Lower Abbey Street. Phone 878 7222

Players Theatre `25 G7`
Trinity College, College Green
Ph 608 2351

Project `25 G7`
39 East Essex St. Phone 881 9613

Tivoli Theatre `24 F8`
135-138 Francis Street. Phone 454 4472

UCD Drama Society `38 K12`
Arts block, Belfield, Dublin 4. Phone 706 8545

MUSIC

Music is very close to Irish hearts and it is almost impossible to visit Dublin without experiencing a musical encounter of one sort or another. From the buskers of Grafton Street and Temple Bar to the pubs and concert halls, there is always somebody close at hand, eager to play a tune or two.

Traditional Irish music remains very popular with locals and visitors alike, and a multitude of pubs have live sessions on a regular basis. Ireland also has a strange love affair with country & western music, but it is in the field of rock and popular music that the Irish have made their presence felt on the world stage in recent years with bands such as U2, the Cranberries, Boyzone and the Corrs, and individuals such as Van Morrison, Bob Geldof, Sinéad O'Connor, Samantha Mumba and Enya, to name but a few.

Dublin is a regular tour stop for these and a host of international recording artists. Most of the big acts play at the Point, but large concerts also take place occasionally at Dublin's three major outdoor sporting arenas, Lansdowne Road, Croke Park and the RDS. There are quite a few good mid-sized venues which include the Olympia Theatre, Vicar Street, Whelan's, the Red Box, and the

Ambassador. The HMV music stores on Grafton Street and Henry Street are good places buy tickets in advance of the show, or try Ticketmaster who have outlets at the ILAC Centre, Jervis Centre and St Stephen's Green Shopping Centre. On a day to day basis, however, Dublin pubs and clubs provide the venues and cater to all musical persuasions, including rock, country, jazz and traditional. For more details, see pages 82-88.

For lovers of classical music, the main venue is the National Concert Hall which is home to the National Symphony Orchestra which plays most Friday evenings. Other performers, both amateurs and touring professionals, take to the stage in the main auditorium throughout the rest of the week. A wide variety of smaller concerts and lunchtime recitals takes place in the adjoining John Field Room which doubles up as the Concert Hall's bar area.

Other venues for classical music include the Hugh Lane Gallery, the National Gallery of Ireland and the Bank of Ireland Arts Centre. If you can't get hold of a free copy of *The Event Guide*, the *What's On* column in the Irish Times is a good place to track down performances. If you prefer the great outdoors, Dublin Corporation sponsor free Music in the Parks on Sunday afternoons during the summer months. Details of forthcoming events are available on the noticeboard in St Stephen's Green.

Dublin, unfortunately, does not have an opera house but Opera Ireland perform two short seasons every spring and autumn at the Gaiety Theatre. Rather ironically, the operatic highlight of the year is the Wexford Festival Opera, which takes place during the last two weeks of October. If you prefer church music, choral concerts and organ recitals are a regular feature at both St Patrick's and Christ Church Cathedrals.

National Concert Hall `31 H9`
Earlsfort Terrace, Dublin 2. Phone 475 1572

Point Theatre `26 J7`
North Wall Quay. Phone 836 3633

Vicar Street `24 F8`
99 Vicar Street. Phone 454 6656

CINEMA

With the help of tax incentives provided by the government, the Irish film industry has managed to establish a niche for itself, with many notable successes such as The Commitments, Brave Heart and Saving Private Ryan. Cinema attendances have soared in recent years and the Irish now go to the 'flicks' as often as anybody else in Europe. The number of screens in and around the city has mushroomed with the opening of several new multiplexes.

Cinema HQ is the Irish Film Centre on Eustace Street which opened in 1992 and is the main outlet for foreign language and arthouse films, although the Screen also does its bit to break the Hollywood monopoly. The IFC is technically a members only club for over-18's, but the reality is that you simply pay €1.27 to be a member for a week, or €12.70 for annual membership. Members are then entitled to buy tickets for up to three guests. Its club status means that uncertified films are occasionally screened as the IFC does not have to submit all of its films to the censor.

Finally, a couple of tips regarding cost. As a general rule, if you want to save a few bob, go to the cinema in the afternoon and you will get in for around two thirds of what it costs in the evening. If you are totally skint, free films are screened outdoors on Saturday nights during July and August in Meeting House Square in Temple Bar. Each film is chosen by an invited celeb who addresses the audience before the film begins. Tickets are available at the Temple Bar Information Centre on Eustace Street. Phone 671 5717.

Classic `30 F10`
Harold's Cross Rd. Ph 492 3324.
2 screens

IMC
Bloomfields Shopping Centre, Dun Laoghaire. Phone 280 7777

Irish Film Centre `25 G7`
6 Eustace St. Phone 677 8788. 2 screens

Omniplex `7 H2`
Santry. Phone 842 8844. 10 screens

Ormonde `38 L14`
Upper Kilmacud Road, Stillorgan. Phone 278 0000. 6 screens

Savoy `25 G7`
Upper O'Connell Street, Dublin 1. Phone 874 6000. 5 screens

Screen `25 H7`
D'Olier Street, Dublin 2.
Phone 672 5500. 3 screens

Stella `31 G10`
207 Lower Rathmines Road, Dublin 6.
Phone 497 1281. 2 screens

Ster Century
Liffey Valley. Phone 605 5700

UCI Blanchardstown
Town Centre, Blanchardstown,
Dublin 15.
Phone 1850 525 354

UCI Coolock `9 M2`
Malahide Road, Dublin 17.
Phone 848 5122
10 screens

UCI Tallaght
The Square, Tallaght. Phone 459 8400.
12 screens

UGC Multiplex `25 G7`
Parnell Street, Dublin 1.
Phone 872 8444.
9 screens

COMEDY

Ireland has produced a rich crop of stand-up comedians in recent years including Ardal O'Hanlon, Sean Hughes, Dylan Moran, Ed Byrne, and Tommy Tiernan, the most recent of several Irish winners of the prestigious Perrier Award at the Edinburgh Festival. It has to be said that most of these acts were actually blooded on the London comedy circuit, but Dublin does have one or two good venues of its own which are helping to keep the production line rolling.

The most established is the International Bar on Wicklow Street (phone 677 9250). Wednesday and Thursday are the main nights for stand-up, Mondays for improv, and there are open mike spots for anybody who wants to make a total eedjit of themselves. Other venues include the Ha'penny Bridge Inn on Wellington Quay (phone 677 0616) which stages a weekly show on Tuesday nights, and the Sugar Club on Lower Leeson Street (phone 678 7188) on Thursday nights. Murphy's Laughter Lounge is no longer with us, but larger scale venues which host some of the bigger acts when they are visiting town include the Olympia, the Ambassador and Vicar Street.

ANGLING

There is fresh water fishing on certain stretches of the River Liffey for salmon, trout, pike and perch. The River Tolka is also popular with trout fishermen and there is some coarse fishing on Dublin's two canals. Fishing permits are available from tackle shops. Howth and Dun Laoghaire are the main centres for sea fishing.

BOWLING

There are several ten pin bowling alleys in and around Dublin, many of which are open 24 hours a day. Stillorgan has the oldest bowling alley in Ireland and it hosts all the major competitions including the Irish Open. Prices depend on the day and time, but the cheapest period is usually before 6pm on weekdays.

Leisureplex
Stillorgan. Phone 288 1656

Leisureplex
Malahide Road, Coolock, Dublin 17
Phone 848 5722

Outdoor bowling greens are in short supply in Dublin, but there's one in Moran Park in Dun Laoghaire and another, which is closer to the centre of town, in Herbert Park in Ballsbridge.

CYCLING

There is a strong cycling tradition in Ireland which was recognised in 1998 when the Tour de France held its first stage in Dublin to honour the international success of Sean Kelly and Stephen Roche. The biggest domestic event is the FBD Milk Race which takes place during the last two weeks of May, starting and finishing in Dublin.

There are no indoor cycling arenas in the city but there is an outdoor track in the Eamon Ceannt Park in Crumlin which is open to the public. Phone 679 6111. If you simply want to hire a bike and do a bit of exploring, there are several bike hire shops in and around the city. See page 66.

GAELIC GAMES

Gaelic football and hurling are Ireland's two national sports, and both have their headquarters at Croke Park which is Ireland's finest sports stadium (phone 836 3222). Both games retain their amateur status and are governed by the Gaelic Athletic Association (GAA) which was founded in 1884 to promote indigenous games. In doing so, its aim was to forge a distinctive Irish identity during a period of British rule in Ireland.

Gaelic football is a fast and physical game, often likened to Australian Rules football which itself evolved from Irish roots, although the Irish play with a round ball. Ireland's 32 counties compete for a place in the All Ireland Final which takes place at Croke Park on the third Sunday in September in front of 80,000 spectators. Tickets for the final are very hard to come by but a trip to one of the earlier rounds at Croke Park will provide a flavour of the event. Parnell Park in Donnycarney is a good place to catch big club games which generally take place on Saturday evenings during the summer months and Sunday afternoons during the winter (phone 851 0650). The All Ireland club finals take place at Croke Park on 17th March, St Patrick's Day.

Hurling is played with a stick and a ball, or *sliothar* (pronounced slitter), and is a game of great skill and co-ordination, despite taking on the appearance of open warfare at times. The All Ireland hurling final is staged on the first Sunday in September, also at Croke Park.

GOLF

Unlike the situation in many other countries, golf is not an elitist game in Ireland. Many of the world's finest courses are close to hand but there are many alternatives to suit players of all abilities. Green fees at the top end of the market can be very expensive, but elsewhere they are rarely prohibitive. Royal Dublin and Portmarnock are two Dublin courses which have long enjoyed international renown, and they have more recently been joined by the K Club in County Kildare, and Druids

Glen and the European Club, both of which are in County Wicklow. Other fine courses in and around the city include Castle, Grange, Hermitage, Island, Malahide, Milltown and Woodbrook. These clubs are all private, but visitors are welcome, especially during the week. Municipal courses offer a cheaper alternative, and there are a number of par-3 and pitch and putt courses dotted around the city. If you want to see how the game really should be played, take a trip to the Irish Open which is one of the leading tournaments on the European Tour, attracting many of the world's top players. The venue changes, as does the timing, but the event is normally staged in early July.

GREYHOUND RACING

Greyhound racing is very popular in Ireland and meetings are staged all year round. Dublin's main venues are Shelbourne Park Stadium on South Lotts Road which stages meetings every Wednesday, Thursday and Saturday night (phone 668 3502); and Harold's Cross Stadium on Harold's Cross Road which stages meetings every Monday, Tuesday and Friday nights (phone 497 1081).

HORSE RACING & RIDING

Ireland is famous around the globe for breeding and training some of the world's greatest thoroughbreds (and it produces a few good horses into the bargain). Many Dubliners enjoy a flutter on the horses and the most convenient place for them to be parted from their cash is Leopardstown Race Course which is only a few miles from the city centre in the suburb of Foxrock (phone 239 3607). The annual highlight is the Hennessy Cognac Gold Cup which takes place in February.

The Irish Grand National is run on Easter Monday at Fairyhouse which is about 15 miles north of the city (phone 825 4877). The headquarters of Irish flat racing is 30 miles south west of Dublin at the Curragh which hosts all five Classics, including the Irish Derby which is a major social occasion. Other courses within an hour's drive of

Dublin include Naas and Punchestown which are both in County Kildare. All national newspapers carry details of the day's race meetings and special buses run from Busaras on race days.

Away from the track, the RDS (Royal Dublin Society) hosts the Dublin Horse Show each year in August. This is a major international show jumping event which attracts hundreds of competitors from around the world and thousands of spectators. If you prefer riding them to betting on them, there are many riding centres in and around Dublin, including Brennanstown Riding School near Bray which offers cross-country rides in the scenic Wicklow Hills, Tuesday to Saturday. For more information, phone 286 3778.

KARTING

Budding Formula One drivers of all ages can hone their skills on indoor circuits. Advanced booking is recommended as karting has become a very popular corporate junket, and the circuits are sometimes entirely booked up for the event.

Kart City
Old Airport Road, Santry, Dublin 9
Phone 842 6322
120 metre indoor track and 1200 metre outdoor track where the karts can reach speeds of up to 80kph. Open Tues-Sun 12noon-10pm.

Kylemore Karting Centre
Kylemore Industrial Estate, Killeen Road, Dublin 10. Phone 626 1444.
Two 360 metre indoor tracks. Open Mon-Sun 11am until late.

RUGBY

The Lansdowne Road in Ballsbridge is the headquarters of the Irish Rugby Football Union - phone 647 3800. The highlight of the year is the Six Nations Championship which takes place during February and March when Ireland take on England, Scotland, Wales, France and Italy. Irish fortunes have been improving recently but, even when there is a conspicuous lack of Irish success on the field, tickets are very difficult to acquire. The thou-

sands of foreign invaders who descend on Dublin for the weekend help to turn these matches into a great social occasion.

SNOOKER

There are quite a few snooker halls in and around the city, the most famous of which is Jason's of Ranelagh (phone 497 5983), home to Ken Doherty, world champion in 1997, and finalist in 2003. A full list of clubs and halls can be found in the Golden Pages.

SOCCER

For many years Irish soccer lived in the shadow of Gaelic games until big Jack (Charlton) came from England, of all places, to manage the national side. Ten years of unprecedented success in the European Championships and the World Cup gripped the nation. Jack returned to his fishing rod and the team was guided by Mick McCarthy to the 2002 World Cup finals, during which time the Irish public was once again seized by the drama, both on and off the pitch. Brian Kerr is currently holding the reins, and there is no sign of interest waning. International matches are played at Lansdowne Road stadium but the headquarters of the Football Association of Ireland are at 80 Merrion Square - phone 676 6864.

The top three Dublin teams are St Patrick's Athletic who play in Inchicore, Shelbourne who play at a small stadium in Drumcondra, and Shamrock Rovers who play at their new stadium in Tallaght. All three teams play in the League of Ireland, usually on Sundays, but support for local league sides is dwarfed by the passionate interest which Dubliners take in the English Premiership.

SWIMMING & WATER SPORTS

If you aren't afraid of cold water, there are good beaches just outside the city at Portmarnock and Malahide to the north, and Bray to the south. Alternatively, the Forty Foot Pool offers a rare opportunity to immerse yourself in both the Irish Sea and Irish literature. Follow in the footsteps of

Gaelic football at Croke Park

Buck Mulligan who went there for a bracing dip in James Joyce's novel, *Ulysses*. The pool, which is named after the 40th Regiment of Foot who used to be stationed nearby, is overlooked by the Joyce Tower and is easily reached by taking the DART to Sandycove. If you aren't feeling quite so hardy, a list of indoor swimming pools can be found in the Golden Pages.

Sailing is a popular activity, especially around Howth and Dun Laoghaire, but sailing clubs are usually restricted to members only. The Irish National Sailing School, however, offers courses for all levels throughout the year. The school is situated by Dun Laoghaire's West Pier - phone 284 4195. Wind surfing is another popular activity in this area of town and equipment and tuition are available from Wind & Wave Water Sports in Monkstown (phone 284 4177).

TENNIS

Since most tennis clubs are privately run for the benefit of members and their guests, the most realistic option is a game in one of the city's parks. There are public courts at Bushy Park in Terenure (phone 490 0320), Herbert Park in Ballsbridge (phone 668 4364) and in St Anne's Park in Raheny (833 1859).

Dublin shops generally open Monday to Saturday from 9am to 6pm, with late shopping in the city centre on Thursday until 8pm. Some city centre department stores and book shops open on Sunday, usually from 12 noon until 6pm. Visitors from outside the European Community can claim a rebate on the purchase price of items carrying Value Added Tax. Inquire at the time of purchase for more details.

Fashion

The English high street invasion has lobotomised much of Dublin's shopping experience, but Irish flair remains in abundance. Busker-friendly Grafton Street is central to any retail therapy, but the total shopping extravaganza that is **Brown Thomas** department store is usually the first stop for any self respecting platinum card holder. The store is filled with five star luxury, but without the snobbishness prevalent in similar emporiums elsewhere. Further up Grafton Street, the Brown Thomas moniker has been shortened to **BT2** to catch those who find street life unbearable without a Prada jacket, Helmut Lang jeans, or Ralph's pony. Cash-strapped wannabees should make their way to the BT-owned **A-wear**. Don't be put off by the uninspiring exterior, for there are treasures to be found within, especially in the designer section.

Carrying on up Grafton Street you can dip into any number of English high street multiples. Ladies of a certain age will enjoy the classic look with a twist at **Pia Bang**, the colourful **Escada, Serena** or the sheer classic look at **Richard Allen**. Foot fetishists can satisfy their desires at elegant **Carl Scarpa, Ninewest,** eclectic **Zerep** and downright tub-thumping **Korky**. At the top is the St Stephen's Green Shopping Centre, thronged with mallrat teenagers and their harassed looking olds. The Dunne family feature prominently in both the broadsheets and the tabloids, but their riches primarily came from **Dunnes Stores**. Its St Bernard brand is not as reliable as its competitor, Marks and Spencer, but there are often very good quality outfits on offer at considerably less cost, and it is certainly worth checking out one of the many branches around Dublin, particularly in the shopping centre. The bilingual labels are not because most of their younger staff are Hispanic, but, because they have opened stores in Spain! If you are an avid bargain hunter, **TK Maxx** on the first floor is a rummagers paradise. Another couple of trendy stores have opened on the first floor, but the ground floor is mostly aimed at the young, street, Popstsars look. Across the road, **Reiss** are now offering a quirky woman's line as well as their established man about town look.

Half way down Grafton Street, Anne Street South is worth a look. **Monica John** and **Aspecto** sit happily together despite their differing target clientele. You need to have stiff mental resolve to pass the Haagen Das shop on Wicklow Street but as that bite on the lips is an inch on the hips you won't want any extra if you like the French chains of **Kookai, Angel** and **Morgan.** Indulge your calorie free fantasies in the French owned **L'Occitane** for luscious smellies. Wicklow Street has become quite stylish with **Sabotage** home to funky boys and riot grrrls, **Buffalo** and **Graham's** shoes, and plenty of coffee shops and cafes. **Patagonia** is the only European outlet for virtuous outdoor types. **Airwave** stock InWear and Adolfo Dominguez and **Ramsay** specialises in clean cut classics. Men are not neglected with **Magee** of Wicklow Street offering corporate man some relaxed dressing, and **Louis Copeland**, seemingly the politicians choice. In adjacent Suffolk Street lies **Avoca**, a rather surreal, Ballykissangel, definitely girlie, shopping experience. Downstairs has a small, decadent food store and sandwich bar and the upstairs cafe is infamous with good reason.

Nassau Street is home to several 'oirish' shops but don't turn back until you have reached the **Kilkenny Design Centre.** Whereas their stock in trade used to focus on lumpy tweed suits and itchy Aran sweaters that appealed mainly to garishly dressed Americans

Powerscourt Townhouse

attempting to return to their roots, the new order epitomises the slick marketing of 21st century Ireland, with a splendid self service restaurant, designer clothing and a range of ceramics and knick knacks which would be at home on the style pages of a Sunday magazine.

West, off Grafton Street, is the exclusive Westbury Mall, behind which lies the Powerscourt Townhouse, a beautifully converted Georgian mansion and courtyard, housing crafts, jewellery, clothing and furniture, as well as some excellent eating houses to stave off the munchies. **The Design Centre** occupies some of the second floor, and the British retail sensation **Karen Millen** has taken up stylish residence on the ground floor. You cannot miss **FCUK**, but make sure you pay attention to some of the other small, innovative retailers around.

Behind Powerscourt, down narrow streets are more Bohemian markets and shops leading onto Great George's Street and Aungier Street. This is an area to watch for the future but, where Bohemia is concerned, Temple Bar still leads the way. On Trinity Street, look out for a branch of **Hobo** if you are into boho, opposite the international chain **Jack Jones** for men. Slip down Dame Lane for **Lara** if you are into Italian designs such as Replay and Versace. Pick up some fresh flowers from **Mad Flowers** on Dame Street - florists to many of Dublin chicest bars and restaurants. Across the road to Temple Bar itself, which is still home to second hand shops, record stores, and the cheaper more 'hippy' look that impoverished Irish students favour. A more hip look is also catered for by the likes of **DV8** on Crown Alley which will kit you out in some very funky footwear. Every fashionista's favourite London shop has come to town-**Urban Outfitters.** Floors of the kitsch, the cool, the funky, the chic, are rounded off by *the* hippest music section, manned by a relaxed and surprisingly affable DJ.

Across the Halfpenny Bridge and en route to pedestrianised Henry Street, on no account call yourself a serious shopper and miss the refurbished **Arnott's**. All the big names are there no matter what your sex or age, including a large concession of the Spanish chain, **Mango**. Liffey Street Upper also offers the surfer look in **Hairy Legs** and the clubby look in **Miss Moneypenny**. Henry Street has fewer tourists, and money stretches a bit further than on Grafton Street. Main outlets of note are the neglected and avoidable ILAC Centre, and the new Jervis Centre with perennial, functional, British favourites including **Debenhams**

and **BHS.** Local hero John Rocha has been lured into the Designers at Debenhams collection. The Moore Street fruit and vegetable market is worth a visit if only to sample a bit of the local banter. **Roches Stores** reputedly is going to have a **Zara** concession when renovations are complete.

Henry Street, with **A-wear, USC** and **Envy** leads out onto O'Connell Street which is not over-endowed with classy shops, but it does have **Penny's,** and the revamped **Clery's** department store along with ear splintering Shuh.

Despite, or perhaps because of, the inexorable rise in Dublin house prices, modern furniture and concept interior design stores have recently become an integral part of the shopping experience, with outlets such as **Haus** on Crow Street and **Foko** on South Great George's Street. Around Essex Street East has become the cool new quarter. Shops such as **Twentieth Century** furniture, **Living**, **Vitra** and **Bulthaup** are serious retail therapy, and have a gallery feel. Your new build apartment demands Scandinavian design from **2cooldesign-home.** If Jade Jagger is your style icon head for **Smock**, but if your taste leans towards Jim Fitzgerald celtic fantasy, **Claire Garvey** is the designer for you. Ornate jewelry and accessories at **Oshun** drag you back onto Dame Street.

Books

Dublin lives up to its literary reputation with a rich selection of book shops, many of which open seven days a week and close later than most other shops. Dawson Street is home to two of the heavyweights, **Waterstones** and **Hodges Figgis**. Around the corner in Nassau Street **Easons** have opened a bright new outlet where Fred Hanna's used to be. **The Dublin Bookshop** on Grafton Street, **Hughes & Hughes** in the St Stephen's Green Shopping Centre, and **Books Upstairs** on College Green are all well stocked and centrally located. **Easons**, with stores on O'Connell Street and throughout Ireland, sell an excellent range of books, newspapers, magazines, stationery, art materials and a variety of other goods. Second hand book shops are too numerous to mention by name but the **Winding Stair** on Ormond Quay rates a mention for the fact that you can enjoy a bite to eat and some good views of the Liffey as well as three floors of books.

Irish Crafts & Textiles

Ireland has a long tradition for producing

Grafton Street - Dublin's College of Retail Therapy

excellent craftware with producers such as Waterford Crystal and Belleek Pottery firmly established in markets all around the world. As mentioned earlier, the **Kilkenny Shop** on Nassau Street has modernised both its stock and its approach in recent years and now ranks as Dublin's leading outlet for Irish craftware. One side of the shop specialises in clothes - mainly woollens, tweeds and linen while the rest of the shop is dedicated to Irish glass, pottery, ceramics and metalwork. The **Blarney Woollen Mills**, also on Nassau Street, follows a similar layout while other outlets noted for their fine selection of Irish woollens are the **Sweatershop** on Wicklow Street and **Dublin Woollen Mills** on Lower Ormond Quay.

The **Crafts Council Gallery** in the Powerscourt Townhouse displays and sells a wide range of crafts by Irish and international designers, and the **Tower Design Centre** on Pearse Street houses a number of studios for craft workers, producing jewellery, ceramics, fabrics, and other hand-crafted items. If your interest is Irish antiques, your first stop should be Francis Street in the Liberties area which provides ample opportunity to browse.

Music

Dublin may be the city of a thousand bands but musical retailing is dominated by British superstores. **Virgin** have one of their Megastores on Aston Quay, and **HMV** have branches on Grafton Street and Henry Street. **Golden Discs**, an Irish chain, have several branches around the city. The Temple Bar area offers some welcome relief from the big players with a growing number of small independent music retailers, many catering to specific tastes. **Claddagh Records** on Cecilia Street, for example, is famous for its collection of Irish traditional and folk music.

Markets

The famous **Moore Street Market**, referred to earlier, operates from Monday to Saturday and specialises in fruit, vegetables and flowers. Across the river, the **Temple Bar Food Market** is held every Saturday in Meeting House Square and appeals more to the stuffed olive brigade with an impressive array of speciality foods on offer. If you are seeking shelter, there is plenty of variety on offer in the covered market in **George's Arcade**, between South Great George's Street and Drury Street. **Mother Redcap's Market** operates on Back Lane near Christ Church Cathedral from Friday to Sunday selling anything and everything from antiques to books and records. Further out of town, **Blackrock** hosts a large market every Sunday which attracts a good crowd to its diverse range of stalls.

Dublin offers many forms of entertainment, but the heart and soul of the city's social life is undoubtedly the pub. There are about one thousand to choose from, and their unique appeal owes much to the wide cross-section of customers they attract.

Many Dublin pubs have changed very little over the past 100 years, and many more have tried to recapture the past, but an increasing number are beginning to look to the future with a strong European influence taking hold around the city. Dublin is arguably the best city in the world for pubs but the primary reason for their allure is the people who work and drink there.

The selection of pubs, clubs and bars below tries to point you in the direction of some of Dublin's finest watering holes but, if you feel strongly that any have been wrongly included or unfairly omitted, feel free to let us know. Most of the pubs listed serve food, and many stage live music. To find out who is playing where, pick up a copy of *The Event Guide*, a free paper published every two weeks and available in many shops, cafés and music venues. Alternatively, invest €2.48 in a copy of *In Dublin* which is similar in nature to London's *Time Out*, and an excellent source of up to date information. If you are on-line, try www.entertainment.ie for reviews and listings.

The list below is NOT broken into categories as so many of Dublin's bars and clubs fall into more than one bracket. Many bars become a nightclub, so that you can carry on drinking until late. When it comes to serious clubbing, however, traditional heavyweights such as the PoD and Rí-Rá, have had their thunder stolen somewhat, now that Spirit has climbed into the ring (see listings).

Opening hours have been omitted as they are often subject to extensions which can vary according to what's on. Pubs normally open from 10.30am to 11.30pm from Monday to Saturday, and from 12.30pm to 11pm on Sunday. Having said that, it has become common practice for most to stay open until 12.30am Thursday to Saturday, and for many to keep serving long after that. Clubs often operate until around 4am. Bear in mind that most pubs raise their prices after 11.30pm.

When it comes to drink, Guinness reigns supreme in Dublin. Brewed at St James's Gate, many Dubliners spend much of their life in search of the perfect pint. Where the Japanese have their tea ceremony, Irish barmen perform their own ritual when pouring a pint of the black stuff but, like all good things in life, it is usually worth waiting for. Competition is increasingly at hand in the form of Beamish and Murphys, both of which are brewed in Cork, but if you prefer a pint of ale or lager, Smithwicks and Harp dominate the market, both brewed by none other than Guinness!

The Temple Bar area has the highest concentration of pubs in the city and it tends to act as a honey pot for tourists, many of whom seem to be enjoying their last hours of freedom, although stag and hen parties have recently been banned by many Temple Bar establishments. If things are getting a bit 'tired and emotional', however, you need only walk a couple of hundred yards to escape the mayhem. As city centre pubs are busy most nights of the week, a hotel bar is often a good bet if you are looking for a quiet drink. Bear in mind, though, that there is no such thing as a quiet drink in Dublin come Friday and Saturday night.

Finally, if you like to keep on the move but aren't sure where you are going, there are some well organised pub crawls. The **Dublin Literary Pub Crawl** is conducted by professional actors who will bring you to a selection of Dublin's best known literary pubs, and enlighten you with performances from the works of Joyce, Beckett and Behan, among many others. The evening kicks off upstairs at the Duke on Duke Street at 7.30pm every night from April to October, at 7.30pm Thursday to Sunday during the rest of year, and at 12noon on Sundays all year round. Tickets cost €10. If you prefer music to literature, The **Musical Pub Crawl** starts at 7.30 pm every night from May to October upstairs at Oliver St John Gogarty's on Fleet Street. The winter schedule is limited to Friday and Saturday nights in November, February, March and April. Tickets cost €10.

If you would rather organise your own pub crawl, then feel free to work your way through the list below!

Aka   `25 G8`
Wicklow Street, Dublin 2
Phone 670 4220
Zen Buddhists would feel very much at home in a few of the newer Dublin bars. None more so than Aka, a large basement which reveals its minimalist tendencies from the moment you descend the wide concrete steps and take in the white walls which have been moulded to give a honeycomb effect. A style bunker offering decent cocktails, funky music and a late bar.

The Bailey   `25 G8`
2-3 Duke Street, Dublin 2
Located just off Grafton Street, The Bailey has an unrivalled literary tradition which stretches back to the mid-19th century. Former patrons include Joyce, Yeats, and Behan, as well as Michael Collins, the evasive IRA General, who drank upstairs while on the run from the British military who were drinking downstairs! The pub no longer trades off these associations, however. Following the redevelopment of Marks & Spencers next door, the refurbished Bailey has dispensed with the literary memorabilia and opted instead for a chic interior which evokes modern Japan more than 19th century Dublin. The clientele are smart and cosmopolitan, and include plenty of Dubliners who like to recover here after a hard day at the office.

The Bank   `25 G7`
22 College Green
Phone 677 0677
The only way to afford an interior like this is to make sure that the bank has already paid for most of it. Retains many of the original features of this former banking hall; mosaic floor, ornate plasterwork, vaulted ceilings and stained glass skylights. Large oval bar dominates the centre of the room, with additional seating on a mezzanine level. Popular stop for shop and office workers after a hard day at the coal face.

The Bleeding Horse   `31 G9`
24 Upper Camden Street, Dublin 2
Phone 475 2705
There has been a pub here since the days of Oliver Cromwell but the current building dates back only to the last century, although the exposed timbers, high ceilings, and the minstrel gallery can conjure up the image of a medieval banqueting hall after a few pints. The pub is popular with nearby office workers, and a good crowd usually takes advantage of the late night bar every Thursday, Friday and Saturday.

One Bank without a liquidity crisis

Bob's `25 G7`
34 East Essex Street, D2. Ph 677 5482
Bob is no longer Bad and his long love affair with country & western music is over. The new Bob has benefited from a rather lavish makeover resulting in a busy groundfloor bar, a relaxed atmosphere among comfy armchairs and sofas on the first floor, and a dance floor to top it all off. Open late.

The Brazen Head `24 F7`
20 Lower Bridge Street, Dublin 8
Phone 679 5186
Located at the end of a cobbled courtyard across the river from the Four Courts, the Brazen Head enjoys the accolade of being Dublin's oldest pub, although its exact age is a matter of some dispute. The pub sign claims the year 1198 but this actually relates to an earlier tavern which used to occupy the same site. A labyrinth of low-ceilinged, smoke-filled rooms makes up the current building which is thought to date back to the early eighteenth century. This is a no frills type of bar, but regular sessions of traditional music help to pull the punters in after dark.

The Bruxelles `25 G8`
7 Harry Street, Dublin 2. Tel 677 5362
An impressive Victorian interior, and a few tables outside if you are hoping to catch a few rays. A prime location, just off Grafton Street, helps to keep things busy both day and night.

Café en Seine `25 H8`
39-40 Dawson Street, Dublin 2
Phone 677 4567
When it first opened in 1993, Café en Seine quickly established itself as many people's favourite Dublin watering hole. Following its recent expansion into the building next door, it has doubled in size but lost none of its appeal. The art deco interior evokes a *fin de siecle* feel, and the air of sophistication helps to attract a discerning, if slightly older clientele. Never fails to impress.

Chief O'Neill's Bar `24 F7`
Smithfield Village, Dublin 7
Phone 817 3860
Smithfield Village is part of a huge urban redevelopment programme which is currently taking place on the north side of the Liffey. Chief O'Neils is part of a complex which includes a hotel and a viewing tower. The bar is modern, spacious and family-friendly with regular performances of live traditional music and dance.

The Clarence Hotel `25 G7`
East Essex Street, Temple Bar
Phone 670 9000

Recovering from a hard day at the office at the Bailey

The Clarence Hotel receives endless free publicity by virtue of the fact that it's owned by the Dublin rock band, U2. The building has undergone major refurbishment since the band took over, but their investment seems to have paid handsome dividends as it is firmly established among the trendiest places in town. If you are out to impress, try the wood-panelled Octagon Bar which caters to a mixture of old rockers and a 'freshly shaken dry martini' crowd.

Cocoon Bar & Cocktail Lounge
Royal Hibernian Way, Dublin 2 `25 H8`
Phone 679 6259
Somewhat similar in feel to the Morrison Hotel, with lots of dark wood, cream walls, comfortable leather armchairs and sofas, and plenty of Dublin's young movers and shakers enjoying the relaxed atmosphere. Great escape from the rigours of Grafton Street on a Saturday afternoon. Late bar Thursday to Saturday.

Dakota `25 G8`
8-9 South William Street, Dublin 2
Phone 672 7690
The stone facade offers few clues to the fact that there's a 'happening' place within. Pile into one of the leather upholstered booths, and quickly forget whether it's day or night in the outside world.

Davy Byrne's `25 G8`
21 Duke Street, Dublin 2
James Joyce immortalised a few Dublin pubs in his time and, yes, this is another one. Described in *Ulysses*, as 'a moral pub', it has has undergone considerable change since it opened in 1873 - physically, rather than morally, of course.

There are now three bars, all refurbished to reflect more modern times, but still retaining a few connections with the past. Davy Byrne, who ran the bar for more than 50 years, appears in one of the murals which were painted by Brendan Behan's father-in-law, no less! The pub's central location, just off Grafton Street, helps to keep it popular with businessmen, shoppers and tourists alike. Look out for Joyce enthusiasts, dressed in Edwardian attire, as they celebrate Bloomsday on 14th June every year.

Doheny & Nesbitt `25 H8`
5 Lower Baggot Street, Dublin 2
Phone 676 2945
Much unimproved! - Nesbitt's is very much the genuine article when it comes to an early Victorian pub, right down to the bare floor boards, smoke stained ceilings, and a bar complete with wooden partitions. Situated around the corner from the Irish Parliament, this is a favourite watering hole for lawyers, politicians and the press pack but it manages to overcome these drawbacks with considerable ease.

The Duke `25 G8`
9 Duke Street, Dublin 2
Phone 679 9553
Characterful pub, just off Grafton Street, and starting point for the Literary Pub Crawl (see page 82).

Excise Bar `26 J7`
Mayor Street Lower, IFSC, Dublin 1
Phone 672 1874
Vaulted stone interior populated by lots of suits from the nearby financial quarter. Cocktail happy hour after work on Thursdays.

The Harbourmaster Bar overlooked by the International Financial Services Centre

Fireworks 25 H7
Tara Street, Dublin 2
phone 648 1099
Zanzibar might well have the longest bar in Dublin, but its cousin, Fireworks, must have the tallest. Housed in what used to be Central Fire Station, the interior is big budget, post-industrial - like something from the set of the movie, *Bladerunner*. A stainless steel spiral staircase rises through three floors which tend to be populated mainly by twenty somethings. DJ's and drinking until late.

Fitzsimons 25 G7
East Essex Street, Temple Bar
Phone 677 9315
A large, split-level bar, designed along

Ron Black's on Dawson Street

traditional lines with bare floorboards and plenty of exposed stonework. Customers include quite a few tourists, as you would expect from a bar set in the heart of the Temple Bar area. For frustrated Riverdance fans, there is a free concert of traditional Irish music, song and dance several nights a week as well as Saturday and Sunday afternoons. Major sporting events are shown on a large screen. The Ballroom Nite Club downstairs caters to those who prefer to dance with both feet on the floor.

Front Lounge 25 G7
Parliament Street, Dublin 2
Whether it's Front Lounge or Back Lounge depends on which entrance you prefer. This is a good place to escape the Temple Bar throng, sink into one of the comfy sofas or armchairs, and cast an appreciative eye over the art, sculpture, and your fellow poseurs. Not a gay pub, as such, but certainly popular with the gay community.

The Gaiety Theatre 25 G8
South King St, Dublin 2. Tel 677 1717
Several Dublin theatres are turned over to late night clubbers on Friday and Saturday nights. The Gaiety makes use of the theatre bars to provide three floors of entertainment with different DJ's and live bands on each floor while cult films are screened in the main auditorium. Doors open at 11.15 pm. The music is mainly salsa, soul, funk reggae & jazz. Bars stay open until 4am. Ground floor Plaza Cafe Bar is open during the day.

The Globe 25 G8
11 South Great George's Street, Dublin 2

Phone 671 1220
One of the first in a long succession of Dublin café bars, but it still attracts a young, up-beat, fashion-conscious crowd. A relaxed atmosphere during the day, becomes more crushed as the evening draws on. Jazz session on Sunday afternoons.

The George 25 G8
South Great George's Street, Dublin 2
Phone 478 2983
Dublin's biggest, and best known gay venue. Bar, club, and a busy schedule of music and entertainment. Other gay pubs include **Out on the Liffey** on Upper Ormond Quay (phone 872 2480), and the **Wig and Pen** on Thomas Street .

Gin Palace 25 G7
Liffey Street Lower
Just along from the Epicurean Food Hall, a lot of money has been spent to make this new pub look old, but the objective has been successfully achieved. A mixed crowd of all types and all ages generate a pleasant hubub.

Gubu 25 G7
8 Capel Street, Dublin 1
Phone 874 0710
A welcome newcomer to a street which is hardly known for trendy watering holes. Both the interior and the clientele could be described as style conscious. Sunday afternoon jazz. By the way, 'gubu' stands for 'grotesque, unbelievable, bizarre and unprecedented' which were the words used by then Prime Minister, Charles Haughey, in reaction to news that a murderer had been discovered in the Attorney General's apartment.

Harbourmaster Bar 25 H7
IFSC, Dublin 1
Phone 670 1688
If you like the contrast of old and new, you will like this place which is set in the old Dock Offices building, bang in the middle of the brand, spanking, new financial district, with acres of steel and glass peering down from above. The dimly lit interior, which has been sensitively converted to its present use, is populated by quite a few of the suits who work nearby, but the atmosphere is very laid back and unpretentious. Decent bar food is available or you can dine in the recently extended restaurant area which overlooks the dock basin outside.

Hole in the Wall 23 D7
Blackhorse Avenue, Dublin 7
Phone 838 9491
Originally a coach house dating back to 1610, the Hole in the Wall is as close as you'll get to finding a pub within the 1700 acres of Dublin's Phoenix Park.

The International `25 G8`
23 Wicklow Street, Dublin 2
Phone 677 9250
A pub of two halves offering a nicely preserved Victorian bar downstairs and a popular comedy club upstairs which also acts as a venue for theatre and live bands. Wednesday and Thursday are the main nights for stand-up, Mondays for improv, and there are open mike spots for anybody wanting to make a total eedjit of themselves. Live music features every other night with rock, traditional, and rhythm & blues bands all appearing regularly.

Irish Film Centre `25 G7`
6 Eustace Street, Temple Bar
Phone 679 5744
Award winning architecture has transformed this Georgian building into a complex which includes two cinemas, a bookshop, and a bar cum restaurant which are all planned around a glass-covered courtyard. Arty clientele with a tendency to wear anything, as long as it's black!

Kavanagh's `17 G5`
Prospect Square, Glasnevin, Dublin 9
Known as the "Gravediggers Arms" due to its proximity to Prospect Cemetery, Dublin's main graveyard and the final resting place of many of Ireland's famous sons. The pub has been in the same family since 1833 during which time its traditional roots have been proudly preserved.

Kehoe's `25 G8`
9 South Anne Street, Dublin 2
Strange to find a Victorian pub just off Grafton Street which has remained largely unchanged and where Dubliners still manage to outnumber tourists. Colour scheme by Nic O'Tene but a good spot to practise the art of conversation.

Lillie's Bordello `25 G7`
Adam Court, Grafton Street, Dublin 2
Phone 679 9204
Probably the most exclusive nightclub in the city. You will have to be on good form to talk your way in on a Friday or Saturday night when it's supposedly "members only". The interior is surprisingly small but celebrity spotting is carried out in considerable comfort, and there's even a table football table to test your late night coordination. Open seven nights a week but things don't get going until after the pubs shut.

The Long Hall `25 G8`
51 South Great George's Street
Dublin 2. Phone 475 1590
Victorian gem which successfully combines the kitsch with the traditional to create a bar which is a real delight. And to cap it all, the staff are friendly and eager to satisfy the thirst of their customers.

McDaid's `25 G8`
3 Harry Street, Dublin 2
Phone 679 4395
Former city morgue, but more famous for being Brendan Behan's local back in the 1950's. Its location, just off Grafton Street, means that the literati are far outnumbered today by tourists and office workers.

Messrs Maguire `25 H7`
1-2 Burgh Quay, Dublin 2
Phone 670 5777
Following in the successful footsteps of the Porterhouse, Messrs Maguire brew their own beer on the premises and serve it up in drawing room comfort. Four spacious floors provide lots of table space, and good views of Dublin can be had from a window seat on the top floor.

The Morrison `25 G7`
Ormond Quay, Dublin 1
Phone 887 2400
A rival of the Clarence when it comes to trendiest hotel in town, the interiors are the work of Ireland's (and Hong Kong's) most famous designer, John Rocha. The ground floor bars offer plenty of posing space among low tables, comfy leather armchairs and suede sofas. Cool space, cool crowd. Late night bar, **Lobo**, is downstairs.

Mulligan's `25 H7`
8 Poolbeg Street, Dublin 2
Phone 677 5582
Mulligan's dates back to 1782 and has changed very little over the years, even retaining its gas lighting. Well known and loved for its slightly dilapidated feel, a lick of paint has recently been applied but it remains essentially a pub with few frills, popular with students and journalists from the two national newspapers located nearby, and revered for the fact that it serves, arguably, the best pint of

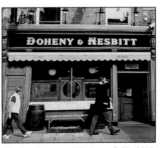

Much unimproved Doheny & Nesbitt!

The timeless Long Hall

Guinness in Dublin. Former patrons include John F Kennedy who used to drop in while working for Hearst newspapers after World War II. There's no shortage of local characters among today's regulars, and the pub has even been immortalised on film, featuring as the local in *My Left Foot*.

Nancy Hand's `24 E7`
30-32 Parkgate Street, Dublin 8
Phone 677 0149
Situated across the river from Heuston Station, Nancy Hands isn't an old bar but it feels authentically Victorian thanks to some extensive and expensive architectural salvage. There are two bars downstairs and a large dining gallery upstairs where you can enjoy decent grub while appreciating the contemporary artwork of Graham Knuttel and Markey Robinson.

Neary's `25 G8`
1 Chatham Street, Dublin 2
Phone 677 8596
Situated close to the back door of the Gaiety Theatre, it is hardly surprising that Neary's is popular with both the acting fraternity and their audiences. The pub is easily recognised from outside by a distinctive pair of brass hands, each holding a glass lamp aloft on either side of the entrance. The ornate interior is Edwardian with a busy bar downstairs and a quieter lounge upstairs. A popular spot to quench a thirst brought on by too much retail therapy.

Ocean `26 J8`
Charlotte Quay Dock, Ringsend, D4
Phone 668 8862
Some things in life are worth seeing, but

The morning after the night before

not worth travelling to see. If you are looking for a waterside setting, and glass fronted, modern architecture, this is for you. Ocean occupies the bottom floor of an upmarket apartment complex, and serves the rapidly expanding office market which is growing up around it. Therein lies the caveat; as the evening wears on, Dubliners either head home or into town, which can leave the atmosphere a little on the quiet side at times.

The Odeon `25 G8`
57 Harcourt Street, Dublin 2
Phone 478 2088
What do you do with an old train station? In this case, convert it, very tastefully, into a bar which feels like it ought to be overlooking Barry's tea plantation. It's not quite Raffles Hotel, but there is definitely an air of faded grandeur, with parquet floors and a cool, art deco interior. Ceiling fans seem almost conspicuous by their absence, but art-lined walls, comfy sofas and armchairs all add much to the laid back air. An outdoor terrace provides an ideal spot to sip a cold drink while contemplating just how good life can be as you watch the helter-skelter of the real world outside. Becomes a nightclub Friday and Saturday nights, when the bar stays open until 3am.

O'Donoghue's `25 H8`
15 Merrion Row, Dublin 2
Phone 676 2807
One of Dublin's best known traditional bars, frequented by musicians, most notably members of the Dubliners. Getting to the bar can be a bit of a challenge if you arrive at a busy time (which is virtually all of the time), but Irish enterprise overcomes such adversity with a strategically placed member of

staff who stands on the counter so that you can shout your order as you come through the door! A courtyard area outside caters for the overspill. Traditional music sessions every night.

The Oliver St John Gogarty `25 G7`
58-59 Fleet Street, Temple Bar
Phone 671 1822
First established in 1850, and later named after the famous Irish surgeon, poet, and politician. Wearing his Senator's hat, it was Gogarty who offered the nation economic hope when he suggested that the crossing of a Friesan bull with a queen bee would result in a country flowing with milk and honey. Customers these days have to make do with a pint of the amber nectar, although a pint of the dark stuff is a more likely tipple. Gogarty's is a popular tourist haunt and you are sure to encounter the occasional stag group. If you are a prospective groom in need of an aphrodisiac, treat yourself to half a dozen oysters! There's also a daily diet of live traditional music, and a musical pub crawl starts upstairs at 7.30pm every evening during the summer months (see page 82). Late bar every night of the week.

O'Neill's `25 G7`
Suffolk Street, Dublin 2
Phone 679 3656
If you have just been to Bord Failte's impressive information centre on Suffolk Street, then it's worth crossing the road to digest all the blurb and plan your itinerary over a pint in O'Neill's. This is a deceptively large, traditional style pub which attracts plenty of passing trade from nearby Grafton Street and Trinity College. Popular carvery lunches.

The Palace `25 G7`
21 Fleet Street, Dublin 2. Tel 677 9290
Palace it may be, but a small one which has changed very little over many years. This is a great little pub with a grand wooden bar, tiled floor and attractive leaded glass. Well worth following in the footsteps of the many literary figures who have passed through its doors and

"Go on, name five famous Belgians!"

now adorn the walls of the back room.

The PoD `25 G8`
35 Harcourt Street, Dublin 2
Phone 478 0166
When the PoD, or Place of Dance, opened in 1993, it quickly became one of Dublin's hippest clubs with style police on the door ready to refuse entry if you fail to make the sartorial grade! Located in two large stone vaults which used to form part of Harcourt Street Rail Station, it still retains its popularity, with international DJ's spinning the discs. Included in the complex are the **Red Box**, a prime venue for live music and club nights, and the **Chocolate Bar**, which is still a comfortable spot to relax with the help of a chocolate vodka and a bit of soul music before going through to the main club.

The Porterhouse `25 G7`
16 Parliament Street, Dublin 2
Phone 679 8847
A pub and micro-brewery laid out on three busy floors. Their own brews are well worth a try, and the food is excellent too, especially when washed down with a pint of Oyster Stout or a glass or two of An Brainblásta! Live music most nights. Late bar Thursday, Friday and Saturday nights.

Pravda `25 G7`
Liffey Street Lower, Dublin 1
It is good to see the north side of the river strike back against the bourgeoisie on the south bank! The truth, or the *pravda*, is that Moscow was never this trendy, with more varieties of vodka behind the bar than you could shake a stick at. There's not much evidence of a Russian theme until you reach the far end of the bar and glimpse the revolutionary murals. The bar upstairs is a bit more chilled out than downstairs but tends not to open until evening time.

Renards `25 H8`
South Frederick Street, Dublin 2
Phone 677 5876
Clubbing seven nights a week with plenty of jazz and blues until the small hours. Has begun to look a little bit frayed at the edges, but there's a dance floor in the basement, a café bar on the ground floor, and a VIP area on the first floor if you feel you warrant it.

Rí-Rá `25 G8`
8 South Great George's St, Dublin 2
Phone 671 1220
Nightclub (pronounced Ree-Raw) where the door policy may be less exclusive than some, but the packed dance floors help to keep the temperature hot. The music includes house, hip-hop and ragga.

Ron Black's 25 H8
37 Dawson Street, Dublin 2
When it comes to good bars and restaurants, Dawson Street is risking an investigation by the Monopolies Commission. Ron Black's threatens to steal the 'best bar in town' mantle from its neighbour, Cafe en Seine. Everything is on a grand scale. The interior is sumptuous, with lots of dark wood panelling and acres of leather, lending the air of a gentleman's club. There are three levels, bags of space, and yet it all manages to remain intimate and sophisticated.

Ryan's 24 E7
28 Parkgate Street, Dublin 8
Phone 677 6097
A fine example of an unspoilt Victorian pub, complete with snugs. Situated near to the entrance of Phoenix Park, regulars argue that Ryan's serves the finest pint in Dublin, a case which is strengthened by the fact that the Guinness Brewery lies just across the river.

The Shelbourne Hotel 25 H8
St Stephen's Green. Phone 663 4500
The Shelbourne may be the city's grandest hotel, but the two ground floor bars are thriving after-work meeting places for many of Dublin's movers and shakers, especially on Friday nights. The smaller **Horseshoe Bar** catches the overspill from the larger **Shelbourne Bar** which has its own entrance in Kildare Street. Both bars, like the rest of the hotel, retain an early 19th century elegance, although you have more chance of appreciating it during the daytime when things are a bit quieter.

Sinnotts 25 G8
South King Street, Dublin 2
Phone 478 4698
Sinnotts is a large basement bar which has been likened to the bar in the TV sitcom, *Cheers*. The decor is quite traditional with a mosaic floor, high beamed ceiling, and panelled walls which are lined with numerous figures from Irish literature. Its location next to the St Stephen's Green Centre helps to keep things busy during the day and late into the night.

JJ Smyth's 25 G8
12 Aungier Street, Dublin 2
Phone 475 2565
By day, JJ's is a no frills affair, a man's pub. A sign behind the downstairs bar which states that 'women aren't served - you have to bring your own' is not displayed entirely in jest. Worthy of a mention, however, due to its status as something of a night time Mecca for jazz and blues enthusiasts. The building was the birth place of the Irish poet Thomas

Café en Seine on Dawson Street

Moore.

Sosume 25 G8
64/65 South Great George's StDublin 2
Phone 478 1590
A lot of cash has been splashed in an effort to create an interior that evokes Japan and the Orient, but the brief does not seem to have been entirely satisfied. Nevertheless, you do get a large, comfortable bar, spread over two floors, in a prime location which ensures that it will never be short of passing trade.

Spi 25 H7
3 Eden Quay
Phone 8746934
If you are finding it difficult to cross the road on O'Connell Bridge, you can always retreat a few yards, and pop into Spi for a pint to steady your nerves. A newcomer to slightly run down Eden Quay, Spi sees itself as a bit of a trend setter and, as such, it attracts an interesting array of customers. One of our contributors happened to find himself sitting at the bar watching Celtic contest the UEFA Cup final, only to be told by an apologetic barman that he had to turn the TV off because poetry evening was about to begin. Both contributor and barman were gutted.

Spirit 25 G7
Middle Abbey Street
Phone 1800 266 399
www.spiritdublin.com
Spirit is the undisputed king of the Dublin dance scene. This is a 1,500 capacity venue which has a lot more to offer than size. The main clubbing space is Body, where the egg-shaped DJ box is flanked on either side by huge screens which display graphic visuals and shots of the dancers below. The ground floor is given over to Soul, another clubbing area, less frenetic than Body, which specialises in disco and funky house music. Around the corner you will find the Holistic centre where you can indulge in a range of alternative treatments, from an Indian head massage to a palm reading. If all this has worked up an appetite, Manna restaurant will take away your hunger. This is a big budget affair, which

attracts many top name performers, and there is no shortage of customers ready to part with €20 to get through the door.

Spy 25 G8
Powerscourt Townhouse Centre
South William Street, Dublin 2
Phone 677 0014
Trendy cocktail bar and nightclub based in three refurbished Georgian rooms.

The Stag's Head 25 G8
1 Dame Court, Dublin 2. Tel 679 3701
A hidden jewel. Built in 1770, the Stag's Head has earned the rare distinction of featuring on an Irish postage stamp. The pub has changed very little since it was remodelled in 1895, with a granite-topped bar, lots of carved mahogany, and eight stained glass windows promoting the stag theme. If you can't get a seat in the main bar, try the back room with its stained glass ceiling. The pub grub is plain, simple and delicious, and includes old favourites such as Irish stew and bacon & cabbage. Downstairs opens at weekends to cope with the extra custom.

Sugar Club 25 H8
8 Lower Leeson Street
phone 678 7188
Just off St Stephen's Green. Looks like an uninspiring 1960's office block from the outside, but was formerly an arts cinema inside. The auditorium feel has been retained, but every second row of banquette seating has been replaced with tables to allow waiter service as you watch live music or comedy on stage. Wood panelled walls, good sound system and a cocktail bar overlooking the serviced area. Caters to over 25's.

The Swan 25 G8
Aungier Street
Feels like a larger version of the Palace -

Terrace drinkers at the Odeon

The Stag's Head - among the very best of the traditional bars in town

a Victorian bar with lots of carved mahogany and wood paneling. Customers are young and old and include quite a few medics from the nearby College of Surgeons.

The Temple Bar `25 G7`
47/48 Temple Bar, Dublin 2
Phone 672 5287
A 19th century stalwart which has seen a few changes in recent years. A modern extension successfully combines old with new, offering two pubs for the price of one, linked by 'The Temple Bar Garden' which is really just a courtyard area where you can catch the afternoon sun while enjoying some pretty decent pub grub. Things get increasingly raucous as the night wears on, and extended opening hours mean that you can grab a late pint and join the throng when many other bars have shut. Irish traditional music on a daily basis.

Thing Mote `25 G7`
Suffolk Street, Dublin 2
An abundance of carved wood helps to make Thing Mote feel like a large confessional and, just for good measure, the far end of the room boasts a gold chandelier which would not look out of place in a Russian Orthodox church. The congregation, mainly Dubliners rather than tourists, pack the pub after work and college.

Thomas Crowe `32 K9`
Merrion Road, Ballsbridge, Dublin 4
A convenient watering hole if you are heading to a match at nearby Lansdowne Road. This is an attractive pub which is proud of its sporting connections judging by the rugby memorabilia which adorn the walls.

Thomas Read/The Oak `25 G7`
4 Parliament Street, Dublin 2
Phone 670 7220
A little bit of Paris, just across the road from Dublin Castle. Lively café bar, good food and great coffee make Thomas Read's a fashionable spot to while away the day or night.

Toner's `25 H8`
139 Lower Baggot Street, Dublin 2
Phone 676 3090
Not far from St Stephen's Green, Toner's is one of Dublin's most characterful pubs, an authentic spirit grocers which concentrates more on the spirits than the groceries these days. Stone floors add to the rustic feel, and some interesting artefacts help to make it the time capsule that it is.

Traffic `25 G7`
54 Middle Abbey Street
Phone 873 4800
Urban chic comes to the north side of the river. Three floors in all, funky soundtrack, young and attractive crowd, late night club Thursday to Sunday. Good place to meet if you are planning to end up in Spirit which is next door.

The Vaults `25 H7`
Harbourmaster Place
Phone 605 4700
What used to be ten Victorian brick-built vaults underneath Connolly Station have been cleverly and tastefully transformed into one of the most impressive eating, drinking and clubbing spaces in town. A slightly peripheral location may pose a problem, however. Opens until late.

The Village `25 G8`
26 Wexford Street, Dublin 2

Phone 4758555
Talk about identity crisis. Formerly Mono, and before that, the Mean Fiddler, but the idea remains the same - modern bar downstairs, and night club upstairs where resident and guest DJ's provide a diet of dance music which pulls in a young crowd.

Viper Room Theatre Bar & Club `25 G7`
5 Aston Quay, Temple Bar
Dublin 2. Phone 672 5566
Intimate bar and club overlooking the river. A small stage at one end of the narrow ground floor bar is just big enough to hold a couple of musicians, usually jazz, salsa, rhythm 'n' blues, while it's DJ and dancing until 3.30am in the club downstairs.

Viva `25 G8`
South William Street
Dublin 2
Glass fronted newcomer, laid out over two floors. Very chilled out atmosphere, and a few seats outside if you want to drink and catch a few rays at the same time.

Whelan's `25 G8`
25 Wexford Street, Dublin 2
Phone 478 0766
An early Victorian pub which is best known as one of the best musical venues in Dublin, staging live performances every night of the week. Rock, blues, and traditional tastes are all catered for, and there's always an enthusiastic crowd of locals and visitors to lap up the entertainment.

White Horse Inn `25 H7`
George's Quay
Not what you might expect from a pub called the White Horse. The interior looks like it might have come from an IKEA catalogue, and the clientele are young and affluent which might have something to do with its proximity to the International Financial Services Centre.

Zanzibar `25 G7`
Ormond Quay Lower
Dublin 1
Phone 878 7212
Zanzibar, along with Pravda just along the road, were pioneers in drawing the Temple Bar crowd across the river although, when you first see inside, you may feel that you have just crossed the Bosphorus rather than the Liffey. The interior seems to have been designed on a 'bizarre bazaar' theme, with palm trees lining a bar so long that it seems to disappear into infinity. It may be a little bit over the top, but the overall effect works extremely well.

There are many hundreds of restaurants and cafés to choose from in Dublin, and this guide attempts to select about 80 of the best. This process is bound to be subjective but no apologies are made for that. After all, how many times have you eaten at a restaurant because it happened to be recommended to you by somebody else?

All establishments featured have been tried out, often frequently, by somebody connected with the Dublin Street Atlas & Guide. They have been selected by people who enjoy good food and drink, bearing in mind price, location and diversity. These places are the ones that we have enjoyed most - the ones that we recommend to friends and relatives. They don't always agree, and perhaps you won't either, but that's what being subjective is all about! Having said that, we would be keen to hear your own recommendations or any objections that you might have regarding any of our choices.

What can be said, without fear of contradiction, is that the restaurant scene in Dublin has been transformed over the past ten years. Choice and quality have improved tremendously, and this trend looks set to continue. In terms of culinary diversity, price and atmosphere, Dublin restaurants can hold their own against most other European capitals.

Many are mentioned in the growing array of good food guides. These publications all have their good points but, invariably, one area of contention is their attempts to estimate the likely cost of a meal. We have all had the experience of going somewhere supposedly "cheap & cheerful" only to find that a couple of drinks and a bottle of plonk end up breaking the bank. On the other hand, there are occasions when you may have taken advantage of a very reasonable fixed price menu, and left with both your conscience and the contents of your wallet largely intact!

When you add in lunchtime and early evening specials, fixed-price menus, and happy hours, attempts to estimate price often tend to be in vain. The system adopted for this guide, therefore, is rather broad-brush in its approach, attempting to categorise a restaurant as expensive, moderate or cheap.

"Expensive" restaurants are those where you can expect the final bill to exceed €40 per head. If you eat somewhere categorised as "cheap", you will, more often than not, escape for less than €20. The final bill at a restaurant falling into the moderate category should fall somewhere between €20 and €40, bearing in mind all the caveats mentioned earlier.

Price Rating

€   **Cheap (usually under €20 per head)**

€€   **Moderate (between €20 and €40)**

€€€   **Expensive (€40+)**

Finally, the golden rule when using this guide is to phone first! All the information included was gathered mid 2003, but restaurants come and go, change ownership, chefs, menus, opening hours and much else, so it's best to check with the restaurant before turning up.

101 Talbot   `25 H7`
100-102 Talbot Street, Dublin 1
Phone 874 5011
Price Rating: €€
Conveniently located for the Abbey and Gate Theatres, Talbot Street seems an unlikely place to go looking for good food, but upstairs at number 101 soon changes that view. The eating space is bright, spacious, and informal while the food is always wholesome and delicious with plenty of choice for vegetarians. *Opening Times: Tues-Sat 5pm-11pm*

Aqua Restaurant   `13 V2`
1 West Pier, Howth
Phone 832 0690
Price Rating: €€€
Situated at the end of a pier, looking out to sea towards Portmarnock, in a building which formerly served as Howth Yacht Club, this is a modern dining room which is difficult to beat for location. The cooking manages to live up to the surroundings, with a strong emphasis on fresh seafood.

Ar Vicoletto   `25 G7`
5 Crow Street, Temple Bar
Phone 670 8662
Price Rating: €€
Simple Italian cooking which allows the flavour of the best, sun-rich ingredients to do the talking. The atmosphere is relaxed and unpretentious, and the prices are relatively inexpensive. *Opening Times: Mon-Sat 1pm-4pm & 6pm-12midnight; Sun 2pm-11pm*

Avoca Café   `25 G7`
11-13 Suffolk St, Dublin 2. Ph 672 6019
Price Rating : €
More chatter per square foot than any other dining room in Dublin, as you will

---

hear when you are making your way up to the top floor of this well known craft-shop. White walls, red leather banquette seating, a light and airy room, and a sea of ladies lunching. The menu is a straightforward selection of healthy salads, panini and one or two home cooked dishes, followed up by some fab desserts. Before you leave the premises, be sure to check out the deli counter and foodhall in the basement. *Opening Times Mon-Sat 10am-5pm; Sun 11am-5pm*

Aya   `25 G8`
49-52 Clarendon Street, Dublin 2
Phone 677 1544
Price Rating: €€
Not unlike London's Yo! Sushi, you can choose to sit at the self-service sushi bar where the dishes pass before you on a conveyor belt, or opt for a table, and select from a menu which is essentially Japanese but with the occasional Irish twist. Cutting edge design, great fun, and food to take away from **Aya Deli** next door. A second Aya Deli has opened recently at the IFSC but, if you remain chained to your desk, you can always order a sushi box on-line (www.aya.ie). *Opening Times: Mon-Sat 12noon-4pm & 5.30pm-11pm; Sun 12noon-10pm*

Bad Ass Café   `25 G7`
9-11 Crown Alley, Temple Bar
Phone 671 2596
Price Rating : €
The Bad Ass, despite some dodgy puns, remains a Temple Bar institution which attracts a predominantly young crowd to its warehouse-style cafeteria. From the bronze hoof-prints on the pavement outside to the pulley system inside which transports your order to the kitchen, there are plenty of quirky touches. The menu suits a tight budget while offering some pretty decent pizzas, pasta, burgers and salads. *Opening Times: Mon-Sun 11.30am-11.30pm*

Bang   `25 H8`
11 Merrion Row, Dublin 2
Phone 676 0898
Price Rating: €€€
Fresh, modern and fashionable - a description which can be applied equally to both the decor and the food and, for that matter, to the staff and many of the clientele. An 'in' place since the day it opened. Early booking essential. *Opening Times: Mon-Sat 12.30pm-3pm & 6pm-11pm*

Bangkok Café   `25 G7`
106 Parnell St
Phone 878 6618
Price Rating: €
There is very little about Parnell Street

Bad Ass Café - a Temple Bar landmark

which could be described as salubrious, but it is an area of rapid change that has certainly become very cosmopolitan in recent years. Every other doorway seems to lead to another internet café. Bangkok Café has been here for quite a few years, and has recently expanded into the premises next door to meet demand at weekends. Don't be put off by the fact that you might have to knock to gain entry; a treat awaits within. The interior looks like it might have come from a beach hut in Phuket, the food tastes authentic, arguably the best Thai nosh in town, prices are cheap, and the service is genuinely warm and friendly. You will come back for more, but remember that you will be asked to pay in cash. *Opening Times: Mon-Sun 5.30pm-10.30pm*

Bella Cuba `32 J9`
11 Ballsbridge Terrace, Dublin 4
Phone 660 5539
Price Rating: €€
Small, upstairs, restaurant where, with the help of a couple of daiquiris and the Cuban jazz soundtrack, you can taste a little bit of Havana without breaking any embargoes. *Opening Times: Mon-Sun 5.30pm-11pm*

Bewley's Oriental Café `25 G8`
78-79 Grafton St, Dublin 2
Phone 677 6761
Price Rating : €
Once Mungo Bewley set foot on Irish shores back in the 1840's, he quickly spotted a gap in the caffeine market, and Bewley's has been a Dublin institution ever since. The flagship outlet on Grafton Street, famed for Harry Clarke's stained glass and the smell of roasting coffee, has recently benefited from a 4m refit. The new regime aims to broaden its appeal and attract more

evening diners, but Bewley's remains at its best as a refuge from the hurly-burly where you can sip your favourite blend of freshly brewed tea or coffee and nibble on something from the mouthwatering selection of home-baked pastries. A table by the window on the first floor Mezzanine still offers an ideal location to watch the world go by while enjoying some good Irish fare, such as smoked salmon on wheaten bread. Look out for the daily lunchtime theatre, and evening cabaret on Thursday, Friday and Saturday. *Opening Times: Mon-Sun 7.30am-11pm (until 12midnight Fri/Sat)*

The Bistro `25 G8`
4/5 Castle Market, off Drury St, Dublin 2
Phone 671 5430
Price Rating: €€
Weather permitting, phone ahead and ask for one of the tables on the outdoor terrace. Then sit back, enjoy some decent bistro fare, and watch the world as it drifts along pedestrianised Castle Market. *Opening Times: Mon-Sat 12noon-11.30pm, Sun 12noon-8.30pm*

Bleu `25 H8`
Joshua House, Dawson Street, Dublin 2
Phone 676 7015
Price Rating: €€€
Latest addition to a rapidly expanding empire which includes **One Pico** and **Pacific**. Has generated one or two murmurs about the timing of such a venture, given the hangover which is currently afflicting the Celtic Tiger. Glass walls reveal an interior which is ultra modern, bordering on minimalist but, like its siblings, the main emphasis is on cooking of the highest calibre. Early signs are that quality will prevail when it comes to keeping the tables occupied. *Opening Times: Mon-Sat 12noon-12midnight*

Bewley's - a Dublin institution since 1840

Bond `25 H7`
5 Beresford Place, Dublin 1
Phone 855 9244
Price Rating: €€
A location at the end of a slightly dilapidated Georgian terrace overlooking the back of Custom House might not be first choice when embarking on a restaurant venture, but Bond is not easily shaken or stirred, and has earned plenty of admirers, especially from the nearby IFSC. The most notable feature is the wine cellar, where you buy a bottle to drink at your table, at retail price plus a modest charge for corkage. The dining room has been nicely updated, the approach is friendly and informal, and the cooking is well managed, like every other aspect of the place. *Opening Times: Mon-Fri 12noon-3pm & 6pm-9pm, Sat 6pm-9pm*

Browne's Brasserie `25 H8`
22 St Stephen's Green, Dublin 2
Phone 638 3939
Price Rating: €€€
As a location, Browne's is top drawer. The richly decorated dining room is situated on the first floor of a Georgian townhouse overlooking St Stephen's Green. The food is familiar brasserie fare but the prices are a little cheaper than you might expect in a setting such as this. *Opening Times: Mon-Fri 12.30pm-3pm & 6.30pm-11pm; Sat 6.30pm-11pm; Sun 12.30pm-3pm & 6.30pm-10pm*

Bruno's `25 H8`
21 Kildare Street, Dublin 2
Phone 662 4724
Price Rating: €€€
Surprisingly contemporary, cellar restaurant situated below Mitchell's wine store. A location close to the heart of government, and a well earned reputation for classic cooking, tends to attract some serious foodies. Also at 30 East Essex Street, Temple Bar (phone 670 6767). *Opening Times: Mon-Fri 12noon-2.30pm & 6pm-10.30pm; Sat 6pm-10.30pm*

Café Irie `25 G7`
11 Fownes Street Upper, Temple Bar
Phone 672 5090
Price Rating: €
The original spirit of Temple Bar lives on at this small, first floor café. Slightly anarchic in appearance but an enjoyable spot to eat an organic breakfast or lunch, and still get change from a tenner.

Captain America's `25 G8`
44 Grafton Street, Dublin 2
Phone 671 5266
Price Rating: €
Planet Hollywood has come and gone, but Captain America fights on with his

armoury of burgers and rock memorabilia which continues to pull in a youthful clientele. *Opening Times: Mon-Sun 12noon-12midnight*

Casa Pasta `13 V2`

12 Harbour Road, Howth
Phone 839 3823
Price Rating: €
A very pleasant setting, overlooking Howth Yacht Club and beyond, a great selection of pasta including lots of seafood options, and all at pretty reasonable prices. The formula has been successfully repeated with the opening of branches in Clontarf (phone 833 1402) and Donnybrook (phone 260 8108). *Opening Times: Mon-Sat 6pm-11pm, Sun 12noon-11pm*

Caviston's `41 S14`

59 Glasthule Road, Dun Laoghaire
Phone 280 9245
Price Rating: €€
Tiny seafood restaurant, next door to Caviston's Deli in Sandycove. Lunch is served in three ninety minute sittings in order to cope with demand. Menu depends on what was caught earlier that day. A local institution, with a large and loyal following - futile to turn up without a booking. *Opening Times: Tues-Sat 12noon-5pm*

Chapter One `17 G8`

18 Parnell Square, D1. Ph 873 2266
Price Rating: €€€
Situated in a vaulted cellar underneath Dublin Writers Museum, Chapter One has benefited from a recent revamp which was deserved after 10 successful years. Over that time, it has built a reputation for *haute cuisine*, and fine wines. There are more than 200 on the list, from a house selection at €20, to a bottle of 1982 Latour at €1,500. With its proximity to the Gate and the Abbey, it is a popular choice for theatre-goers, some of whom come early for a starter and main course, and return after the show for dessert. *Opening Times: Tues-Fri 12.30pm-2.30pm & 6pm-11pm; Sat 6pm-11pm.*

Chili Club `25 G8`

1 Anne's Lane, Dublin 2
Phone 677 3721
Price Rating: €€
Tucked away, just off South Anne Street, the Thai chefs at the Chili Club ensure that the food is authentically hot and spicy, yet easy on the palate. *Opening Times: Mon-Sat 12.30-2.30 & 6pm-11pm; Sun 6pm-11pm*

China-Sichuan Restaurant `38 L14`

4 Kilmacud Road Lower

Bleu - a newcomer to Dawson Street

Phone 288 4817
Price Rating : €€
Despite an uninspiring setting in the suburb of Stillorgan, this is Chinese food worth going that little bit out of your way for. The chefs, like many of the ingredients, are from Sichuan province in western China and the cooking delivers an authentic taste characterised by strong flavours (chilies are an essential ingredient in many Sichuan dishes). *Opening Times: Mon-Fri/Sun 12.30-2.30; Mon-Sun 6pm-11pm.*

Cornucopia `25 G8`

19 Wicklow Street, Dublin 2
Phone 677 7583
Price Rating: €
Popular vegetarian restaurant serving a wide selection of imaginative dishes at very reasonable prices. *Opening Times: Mon-Sat 8.30am-8pm (until 9pm Thurs).*

Cruzzo

Marina Village, Malahide
Phone 845 0599
Price Rating: €€€
Grand scale, 250 seater restaurant which would not look out of place in Marbella, although it actually overlooks the cooler waters of Malahide Marina. Cruzzo represents an investment of €3m-€4m, and for that money you get contemporary cooking and a fair degree of style and comfort, which has proved popular with the business and political fraternity. *Opening Times: Mon-Sun 12.30pm-2.30pm & 6pm-10.30pm*

Dish `31 H9`

146 Upper Leeson Street, Dublin 4
Phone 664 2135
Price Rating: €€€
The original outlet in Temple Bar is sorely missed, but an elegant set of rooms in a smart new location brings it closer to its natural customer base. Remains one of the most fashionable restaurants in town. The cooking is bang up to date, the food beautifully presented, and the service invariably friendly and efficient. *Opening Times: Mon-Sun 12noon-4pm & 6pm-11pm*

Dunne & Crescenzi `25 H8`

South Frederick Street, Dublin 2
Phone 677 3815
Price Rating: €
For some, Italy is all about Prada, Gucci, and D&G. D&C, on the other hand, specialise in bringing authentic *eneteca* atmosphere to Dublin. Their burgeoning empire is based on rustic good looks, deli style food, and heart warming wine by the glass or bottle. Two outlets on the same street, both crammed for most of the day. *Opening Times: Mon 8.30am-7pm, Tues-Sat 8.30am-11pm*

Eden `25 G7`

Meeting House Square, Temple Bar
Phone 670 5372
Price Rating: €€€
This is no shrinking violet. The contemporary design exudes self-confidence, and the outdoor terrace overlooking the square immediately alerts you to the fact that this is somewhere cool and hip. Not as 'in' a place as it once was perhaps, but consistently high standards of cooking and service help to ensure that its premier league status is retained. *Opening Times: Mon-Sun 12.30pm-3pm & 6pm-10.30pm*

Elephant & Castle `25 G7`

18 Temple Bar, Dublin 2
Phone 679 3121
Price Rating : €€
American style cooking served up in bright, informal surroundings by friendly staff - the combination is familiar, but nowhere else in Dublin has achieved such a successful blend, judging by the busy atmosphere which lasts the whole day long. The house speciality is the "elephantburger", but alternatives include an exhaustive selection of

Bruno's - below Mitchells Wine Merchants

Ely Wine Bar on Ely Place

omelettes, and some excellent salads and pasta dishes. The legendary spicy chicken wings make a delicious starter but the portion seems to be designed to satisfy the appetite of a Texan oilman, so it might be a good idea to share. Reservations are not accepted, but you can put your name on a waiting list if there are no tables free, and pop over the road for a drink while you're waiting. *Opening Times: Mon-Fri 8am-11.30pm, Sat 10.30am-11.30pm, Sun 12noon-11.30pm*

Ely Wine Bar `25 H8`
22 Ely Place
Phone 676 8986
Price Rating: €
If you are after a single plate of something to satisfy your taste buds, and a glass or two of your favourite tipple to wash it down, then this is the place for you. It occupies the ground floor of a Georgian townhouse, plus a bigger and more convivial basement area. The wine list is extensive, more than 70 wines available by the glass, and the staff are knowledgeable and only too happy to share their opinions with you. *Opening Times: Mon-Sat 12noon-3pm & 6pm-10pm.*

Epicurean Food Hall `25 G7`
Liffey Street Lower
Price Rating: €
Such a good idea, it's a surprise that it took so long to materialise. A multitude of eateries and gourmet food and wine shops under the one roof. A couple of highlights are **Oppermann** (Formerly C-Bar) which specialises in simply cooked seafood, although steak is now an option following the recent change of identity. **Miss Sushi**, as you might expect, offers

a delicious range of freshly made sushi, mainly to take away, but it is possible to eat on the premises. Open normal shopping hours.

Fitzers `25 G8`
51 Dawson Street, Dublin 2
Phone 677 1155
Price Rating: €€
Fitzers have several branches around the city and all are recommended for their tasteful interiors and their ability to deliver interesting food at sensible prices. Dawson Street offers a bright and sunny decor, in keeping with the Cal-Ital style of cooking, and outdoor seating which is usually occupied by ladies who like nothing better than to lunch. Other branches are on Temple Bar Square (679 0440) and in the National Gallery on Merrion Square West. *Dawson Street Opening Times: Mon-Sun 11.30am-11pm*

The Forty Foot `41 R13`
Pavilion Centre, Dun Laoghaire
Phone 284 2982
Price Rating: €€€
Named after a well known local bathing place, this is a two storey bar and restaurant in the recently developed Pavilion. The first floor restaurant achieves a balance between a striking designer interior, and egalitarian seating arrangements which afford every table a stunning sea view over Dun Laoghaire harbour and Dublin Bay. Worth coming for the setting alone, but the modern European cuisine holds its own, as does the service and overall ambience.

The French Paradox `26 J8`
53 Shelbourne Road, Dublin 4
Phone 660 4068
Price Rating: €
Ballsbridge is home to an increasing number of trendy delis which cater to the sort of palate which can distinguish between virgin and extra virgin olive oil. The French Paradox is a wine shop with a small dining area and deli counter upstairs. It is an absolute treat to secure a table, and share a couple of their Mediterranean style platters of Spanish hams, Italian antipasti, cured fish, patés

Eden on Meeting House Square

and cheeses, all complemented by a superb choice of wines by the glass. A place that delights in the quality of their food, wine, service, and general ambience. *Opening Times: Mon-Sat 12noon-3pm & 5pm-9.30pm, Sun 5pm-9.30pm*

Fresh `25 G8`
Powerscourt Centre, Dublin 2
Phone 671 9669
Price Rating: €
If your body is a temple and your pockets are not as deep as they might be, Fresh will provide you with a wholesome range of soups, sandwiches, veggie meals, herbal teas and juices, without inflicting much financial damage. *Opening Times: Mon-Sat 9am-6pm (until 8pm on Thursdays)*

Gotham Café `25 G8`
8 South Anne Street, Dublin 2
Phone 679 5266
Price Rating: €
New York theme café which is always buzzing, partly due to it's location just off Grafton Street, but mainly because its customers keep coming back to sample the gourmet pizzas, interesting pastas and salads, and the warm and friendly atmosphere. *Opening Times: Mon-Sat 12noon-12midnight; Sun 12noon-10.30pm*

Govinda's `25 G8`
4 Aungier Street, Dublin 2
Phone 475 0309
Price Rating: €
Hippy chic. Extremely cheap vegetarian restaurant run by Hare Krishna. No pressure to sign up for a haircut and Tibetan robes though, so go ahead and enjoy great value curries, kebabs and burgers. *Opening Times: Mon-Sat 12noon-9pm*

Halo `25 G7`
Morrison Hotel, Ormond Quay
Phone 878 2999
Price Rating: €€€
Since it opened, the Morrison has been vying with the Clarence for title of 'trendiest hotel in town'. John Rocha was enlisted to put his mark on the interiors and, as one would expect, the hotel restaurant, Halo, is very much a designer space; split level, high ceilings, lots of dark wood, bordering on minimalist. The fusion cooking is highly rated and combines with the space to attract a suitably fashion conscious crowd. *Opening Times: Mon-Sun 12.30pm-2pm & 7pm-10.30pm*

Il Baccaro `25 G7`
Meeting House Square, Dublin 2
Phone 671 4597
Price Rating: €€

Meeting House Square may be Dublin's newest piazza, but Il Baccaro conjures up images of a medieval drinking vault in the bowels of Prague. Don't be deceived by the dimly lit interior, however, because this is a place to have fun, with good humoured Italian staff on hand to keep the warm house red flowing by the carafe. The food is plain and simple, the prices are affordable and, if you prefer life above ground, there are a few tables outside in the summer. *Opening Times: Mon-Fri 6pm-11pm, Sat 12noon-11pm, Sun 6pm-11pm*

Imperial Chinese `25 G8`
12a Wicklow Street, Dublin 2
Phone 677 2580
Price Rating: €€
Enjoyable Cantonese cuisine every day of the week, but Sunday tends to be when members of the Chinese community arrive in force to partake of the legendary dim sum. *Opening Times: Mon-Sun 12.30pm-11.30pm*

Independent Pizza Company `17 H5`
28 Lower Drumcondra Rd, Dublin 9
Phone 830 2044
Price Rating: €
Has recently moved a few doors along to smarter premises on the airport road, but remains a busy, friendly, local pizzeria which has been serving some of the tastiest pizzas in town since 1984. *Opening Times: Sun-Thurs 12noon-12midnight (until 10.30pm Sundays)*

Jacob's Ladder `25 G8`
4-5 Nassau Street, Dublin 2
Phone 670 3865
Price Rating: €€€
Elegant, upstairs restaurant overlooking the grounds of Trinity College. Seafood features prominently on the menu and the imaginative mix of classic and modern cooking is rated among the best in town. *Opening Times: Tues-Sat 12.30pm-2.30pm & 6pm-10pm*

Jaipur `25 G8`
41 South Great George's Street, Dublin 2
Phone 677 0999
Price Rating: €€
No flock wallpaper here. Light and modern setting matched by a contemporary approach to Indian cooking. A second outlet in Dalkey (phone 285 0552). *Opening Times: Mon-Sun 5.30-11.30pm*

Kaffe Moka `25 G8`
39 Sth William Street
Phone 679 8475
Price Rating : €
Kaffe Moka has long been one of the most popular coffee houses in Dublin with facilities that include a library and

The Elephant & Castle in Temple Bar - one of the most popular restaurants in town

games room on the second floor. Another branch at the Epicurean Food Hall helps to satisfy customer demand.

Kilkenny Restaurant & Café `25 H8`
6 Nassau Street, Dublin 2
Phone 677 7066
Price Range : €
Situated on the first floor of the Kilkenny Shop, famous for its range of Irish clothing and craft goods, the dining area is modern and spacious. A good range of wholesome lunches are on offer, backed up by an interesting variety of home baked breads, cakes and biscuits which you can buy to eat in or take away. Join an endless stream of hungry shoppers and office workers, and try to get a table by the window where you can gaze into the more peaceful world of Trinity College. *Opening Times: Mon-Sat 9am-5pm (until 7pm on Thurs), Sun 11am-5pm*

King Sitric `13 V2`
East Pier, Howth
Phone 832 5235
Price Rating: €€€
When you arrive in Howth for the first time you will find it difficult to believe that you are only 20 minutes from the centre of Dublin. Set in an old harbourmaster's house, the King Sitric has recently been refurbished to take full advantage of the spectacular views over Balscadden Bay. The menu is dominated by whatever the Howth fishing fleet manages to catch earlier that day - the restaurant even has its own lobster and crab pots - but alternatives are available if you prefer meat to fish. An impressive ground floor wine cellar, and well appointed overnight accommodation (8 bedrooms) complete the new look.

Opening Times: Mon-Fri 12.30pm-2.30pm & 6.30pm-10.30pm; Sat 6.30pm-10.30pm

La Corte `25 G8`
Powerscourt Townhouse Centre
Price Rating: €
Part of **Dunne & Crescenzi's** Italian empire, La Corte delivers another slice of *la dolce vita* on the top floor here, and at the Epicurean Food Hall. Arrive early for lunch to secure a table with a bird's eye view of the goings on below.

La Maison des Gourmets `25 G8`
15 Castle Market, off Drury St,Dublin 2
Phone 672 7258
Price Rating: €
Ground floor boulangerie where the smell of freshly baked bread fills the air, and small first floor café where you can sample the produce not long after it has

Browne's Brasserie on St Stephen's Green

Diners enjoying some Asian Fusion at Mao

left the oven. Soups, warm open sandwiches, salads and a selection of cured meats. *Vive la France! Opening Times; Mon-Sat 8am-6pm.*

La Stampa `25 H8`
35 Dawson Street, Dublin 2
Phone 677 8611
Price Rating : €€€
The dining room at La Stampa started life as the ballroom of a 19th century guildhall and the decor retains much of the original grandeur. The international cuisine occasionally struggles to live up to the impressive setting, but the bustling atmosphere is difficult to resist - an ideal place to see and to be seen. *Opening Times: Mon-Fri 12.30pm-2.30pm; Mon-Sun 6pm-12midnight*

L'Ecrivain `25 H8`
109a Lower Baggot Street, Dublin 2
Phone 661 1919
Price Rating: €€€
Some restaurants serve great food but lack atmosphere (the late, lamented Commons, for example). Others are let down by erratic service. L'Ecrivain, however, excels on all fronts. There is always a buzz, a lot of suits at lunchtime, but an interesting mix of business and pleasure is generally the order of the day. They come for modern Irish cooking at its best, generous portions, and service which is not too formal, just spot on. Brilliant. *Opening Times: Mon-Fri 12.30pm-2pm; Mon-Sat 7pm-11pm*

Lemon Crepe Co `25 G8`
66 South William Street, Dublin 2
Phone 672 9044
Price Rating: €
Tiny pancake joint, easily identified by the lunchtime queue for its cheap and delicious crepes.

Leo Burdock's `25 G8`
2 Werburgh Street, Dublin 8
Price Rating : €
There's no seating at Burdock's but it is worthy of a mention as it has been here since 1913 and serves arguably the best fish and chips in Ireland! The park down the road beside St Patrick's Cathedral is a good place to sit in judgement. *Opening Times: Mon-Sun 12noon-12midnight*

Les Frères Jacques `25 G7`
74 Dame Street, Dublin 2
Phone 679 4555
Price Rating: €€€
Situated across the road from Dublin Castle and next to the Olympia Theatre, Les Frères Jacques is one of Dublin's 'old school' restaurants, serving classic *haute cuisine* in a setting which is unmistakably French. The menu takes advantage of a ready supply of fresh seafood, and the ambience is equally well suited to doing business or celebrating a special occasion. *Opening Times: Mon-Fri 12.30pm-2.30pm & 7.30pm-10.30pm; Sat 7.30pm-10.30pm*

Mao `25 G8`
2-3 Chatham Row, Dublin 2
Phone 670 4899
Price Rating: €€
Very hip café bar serving oodles of noodles and much more besides. They describe it as Asian Fusion, which means that much of the food is quite hot and spicy, so it might be wise to order a cold Asian beer to help cool the taste buds. Forever busy, the successful formula has been repeated at a new outpost in the Pavilion in Dun Laoghaire (phone 214 8090). *Opening Times: Mon-Sun 12noon-11pm*

Mermaid Café `25 G7`
69/70 Dame St, Dublin 2
Tel 670 8236
Price Rating: €€€
Smallish restaurant with a decor which looks like it was inspired by New England Shakers and a menu which is

The Morrison Hotel - home to Halo

not without some American influence as well. A popular place since the day it opened. Great food, complemented by a fine wine list and very personable service. Top place for Sunday brunch. *Opening Times: Mon-Sat 12.30pm-2.30pm & 6pm-11pm; Sun 12noon-3.30pm & 6pm-9pm*

Milano `25 G8`
38 Dawson Street - phone 670 7744
19 East Essex Street - phone 670 3384
Price Rating: €€
British chain, Pizza Express, prefer to operate in Dublin under the assumed name of Milano. What you get, however, is very much as you would expect - well chosen locations, designer interiors, pleasant service, a smart young crowd, and pizzas which are as good as you'll find anywhere in Dublin. For those of us who would prefer a wider choice of pasta on the menu, Pasta Di Milano on Ormond Quay has helped to fill the gap. *Opening Times: Mon-Sun 12noon-12midnight*

Mimo `25 G8`
Powerscourt Townhouse, South William St, Dublin 2
Phone 679 4160
Price Rating: €
Mimo, which occupies most of the ground floor of the recently refurbished Powerscourt Townhouse, offers one of the most impressive spaces in the city to enjoy coffee, a snack, or a bite of lunch. The sort of place where you meet for coffee and end up drinking champagne. You will only have to stagger a few more yards to make it down the steps of **bá mizu,** Mimo's new sister, a bar and seafood bar housed in an impressive set of stone vaulted rooms.

Monty's of Kathmandu `25 G7`
28 Eustace Street, Temple Bar
Phone 670 4911
Price Rating: €€
Mouthwatering Nepalese cooking washed down by their own Shiva beer, in this cosy little restaurant in the heart of Temple Bar. Opening Times: Mon-Sat 12noon-2.30pm & 6pm-11.30pm, Sun 6pm-11pm

Munkberry's Restaurant
22 Castle Street, Dalkey
Phone 284 7185
Price Rating: €€€
Dalkey village is one of Ireland's most fashionable addresses, shared by the likes of Damon Hill and Enya. Munkberry's is a bistro in harmony with its location - small, stylish and great. The menu has a Mediterranean flavour, the food nicely cooked and presented,

and the atmosphere lively and in keeping with a restaurant which enjoys a strong local following.

Nude `25 G8`
21 Suffolk Street, Dublin 2
Phone 672 5577
Price Rating: €
This is nudity which concentrates more on the organic than the orgasmic, although their range of fresh soups, hot and cold tortilla wraps, freshly squeezed juices and smoothies may well leave you with a feeling of warmth and satisfaction. Take away, or pull up a piece of bench and park yourself at one of the large communal tables. A second outlet has opened recently on Lower Leeson St. *Opening Times: Mon-Sat 8am-10pm; Sun 11am-7pm.*

One Pico `25 H8`
Molesworth Place, Dublin 2
Phone 676 0300
Price Rating: €€€
Hidden down a narrow laneway, but painted sunshine yellow to make up for it, stands Eamonn O'Reilly's flagship restaurant. Premier league food and impeccable service in an intimate setting (the waiters have to pass single file between tables). A place to celebrate birthdays, anniversaries, or just the joy of eating. Best not to bring the mistress though, as this is the realm of politicians, journalists and businessmen who enjoy conspicuous consumption. Excellent wine list to complement fine Irish cooking, and a cheese board to die for. *Opening Times: Mon-Sat 12.30pm-2pm & 6pm-10pm.*

Pacific `25 G7`
17-19 Sycamore Street, Dublin 2
Phone 677 4199
Price Rating: €€
Relative newcomer, occupying a large space which was formerly home to Belgo. The look is cool and stylish, not unlike one or two of the customers, and the fresh and contemporary approach to the cooking lives up to the high standards one has come to associate with its siblings, One Pico and Bleu. *Opening Times: Mon-Sun 12noon-3pm & 5pm-11pm*

Panem `25 G7`
21 Lower Ormond Quay, Dublin 1
Phone 872 8510
Price Rating: €
Tiny Italian style bakery and coffee bar which serves fantastic breads and pastries as well as a few lunchtime dishes, all to eat in or take away. If space is at a premium, head across the road to one of the benches overlooking the river on the

Great pizzas at Milano on Dawson St

Liffey boardwalk. *Opening Times: Mon-Sat 9am-5pm; sat 9am-5.30pm*

Pasta Fresca `25 G8`
2-4 Chatham St, D2. Phone 679 2402
Price Rating : €€
Despite the long opening hours, Pasta Fresca always seems to be bursting at the seams but the staff are well drilled and they tend to cope with ease. You won't be surprised to learn that fresh pasta is the house speciality, but there's a full Italian menu to choose from, and prices are reasonable. *Opening Times: Mon-Sat 11am-11.30pm; Sun 12noon-10pm*

Queen of Tarts `25 G7`
4 Cork Hill, Dame St, Dublin 2
Price Rating: €
Small tea room which produces some wonderful, and cheap, home baking. *Opening Times: Mon-Fri 7.30am-6pm, Sat 9am-6pm, Sun10am-6pm*

Rajdoot `25 G8`
26-28 Clarendon Street, Dublin 2
Phone 679 4274
Price Rating : €€
Situated behind the Westbury Hotel, the Rajdoot is one of Dublin's oldest and finest Indian restaurants. Tandoori cooking is the house speciality, but there are some interesting alternatives to chicken including breast of duck, several fish dishes and a good selection of vegetarian options, all served up in opulent surroundings. *Opening Times: Mon-Sat 12noon-2.30pm & 6pm-11pm, Sun 1.30pm-11pm*

Restaurant Patrick Guilbaud `25 H8`
21 Upper Merrion Street, Dublin 2
Phone 676 4192
Price Rating : €€€+
This is the prize heavyweight (or coq of the walk!) of Dublin's French restaurants. The food takes advantage of a ready supply of fresh Irish ingredients, but the cooking is rigorously French and qualifies for a mention in all of the good food guides (Guilbaud's was the first restaurant in Ireland to be awarded two Michelin stars). Such a pedigree, however, comes at a price. Although there are some reasonably priced set menus, this is the land of expense account dining - so, if you intend paying by cash, be careful not to fall off your wallet when you sit down. *Opening Times: Tues-Sat 12.30pm-2.15 & 7.30pm-10.15pm*

Roly's Bistro `32 J9`
7 Ballsbridge Terrace, Dublin 4
Phone 668 2611
Price Rating: €€€
When it opened back in 1992, Roly's quickly became one of the most popular places in town. The fact that it has remained so owes much to the high standards of cooking and service, as well as a fashionable location close to the American embassy and RDS. The menu may change but the food is always beautifully prepared, keenly priced, and served up in a very relaxed atmosphere. *Opening Times: Mon-Sun 12noon-3pm & 6pm-10pm*

Shanahans on the Green `25 G8`
119 St Stephen's Green, Dublin 2
Phone 407 0939
Price Rating: €€€+
If you hail from Texas and find it difficult to comprehend how an eight ounce morsel of steak could possibly constitute a full meal, then you have landed on your feet here. Decidedly upmarket, American style steakhouse, serving anything up to 32 ounces of Irish Angus beef, although there are plenty of alternatives to steak if you are not into red meat. *Opening Times: Mon-Sun 6pm-10.30pm*

Soup Dragon `25 G7`
168 Capel St, Dublin 1.
Phone 872 3227

One Pico on Molesworth Place

Mimo at the Powerscourt Townhouse

Price Rating: €
Tiny soup kitchen. The menu changes regularly, but there are about a dozen freshly made soups to choose from, and they come in three sizes, with bread and a piece of fruit thrown in (not literally). *Opening Times: Mon-Fri 8am-5.30pm; Sat 11am-5pm*

Steps of Rome   `25 G8`
1 Chatham Street, Dublin 2
Phone 670 5630
Price Rating: €
Small, one roomed, diner staffed by Italians who know a thing or two about how to make a proper espresso, delicious pasta, and scrumptious pizza which comes by the slice. Seats are at a premium but prices are bargain basement. A second outlet has opened recently on St Andrew's Lane close to Dublin Tourism, but it lacks the warmth and intimacy of the original. *Opening Times: Mon-Sat 12noon-11pm, Sun 1pm-10pm*

The Tea Room   `25 G7`
Clarence Hotel, Wellington Quay, D2
Phone 670 9000
Price Rating: €€€
One of the coolest restaurants in town, and certainly a good choice if you are out to impress a prospective partner (in love, or in business). The modern cooking combines effortlessly with the elegant art deco surroundings, and the service is discreet but attentive. *Opening Times: Mon-Sun 12.30pm-2.30pm & 6.30pm-10.30pm*

Thornton's   `25 G8`
128 St Stephen's Green, Dublin 2
Phone 478 7008
Price Rating: €€€+
Thornton's has moved from its old home in Portobello to a large second floor space overlooking St Stephen's Green.

Decor wise, it's modern and light, with 40 shades of cream if you include the art collection. Kevin Thornton's cooking has received many accolades and awards. The combination of French *haute cuisine* and a seemlessly run operation does not come cheap, but many people will go far out of their way to eat here. Perhaps that is its only weakness - the reverence shown towards the food can sometimes contribute to a slightly rarefied atmosphere.*Opening Times: Tues-Sat 12.30pm-2pm & 7pm-10.30pm*

Tribeca   `31 H9`
65 Ranelagh
Phone 497 4174
Price Rating: €€
Suburban sister to Dish. Lots of straightforward stalwarts on the menu, including chicken wings and burgers, but plenty of interesting alternatives and an ever changing specials board. Busy throughout the day. *Opening Times: Mon-Sun 12noon-11pm*

tri.D   `25 H8`
Dawson Street, Dublin 2
Price Rating: €
Foodwise, it's panini, wraps and salads, served up in a pretty basic café setting, but where else can you order in the mother tongue? Staff speak Irish as a first language but, if you are rusty or incapable, English will be accommodated! *Opening Times: Mon-Fri 9am-7pm (until 8pm on Thursdays), Sat 11am-6pm*

Trocadero   `25 G8`
3 St Andrew Street
Phone 677 5545
Price Rating: €€
One look at the richly decorated interior and the rogues gallery of luvvies that adorn the walls, and it should come as no surprise to learn that the Trocadero enjoys a long and close association with nearby theatre land. The food is traditional and straightforward, but the secret of its enduring popularity has more to do with the fact that the Troc is a great place to socialise, often long into the night, once the show is over. *Opening Times: Mon-Sat 5pm-12midnight*

Epicurean Food Hall on Lower Liffey St

Unicorn   `25 H8`
off Merrion Row, Dublin 2
Phone 676 2182
Price Rating: €€
Busy trattoria which benefits from an outdoor terrace and a secluded setting somewhat reminiscent of a Chelsea mews. *Opening Times: Mon-Sat 12.30pm-3.30pm & 6pm-11pm*

Wagamama   `25 G8`
South King Street, Dublin 2
Phone 478 2152
Price Rating: €
Part of a London-based chain of Japanese noodle bars which base their success on a designer cool, minimalist, interior where diners sit at long communal tables and choose from an excellent range of reasonably priced rice and noodle dishes. Quirky touches include a hand-held electronic device used by the waiting staff to radio your order through to the kitchen. *Opening Times: Mon-Sat 12noon-11pm; Sun 12noon-10pm*

The Winding Stair   `25 G7`
40 Lower Ormond Quay, Dublin 1
Phone 873 3292
Price Rating : €
Cafe situated on the top floor of one of Dublin's oldest bookshops. The feel is that of a workers' co-operative but the soups, sarnies, salads & cakes are all as enjoyable as the grandstand view over the Liffey. *Opening Times: Mon-Sat 9.30am-6pm; Sun 1pm-6pm*

Yamamori   `25 G8`
71-72 South Great George's Street
Phone 475 5001
Price Rating : €€
Yamamori is a fun place to eat at relatively low prices. The portions are generous and the Japanese cooking is full of flavour with plenty of choice for vegetarians. Noodles are the speciality of the house - they come stir-fried or in a soup, with a multitude of additional ingredients to add taste and texture. If you aren't a fan of noodles, there are plenty of sushi, tempura, and chargrilled meat and fish options to choose from. *Opening Times: Mon-Sun 12.30pm-11pm*

Zaytoon   `25 G7`
Parliament Street
Price Rating: €
If you need some in-flight refueling, but don't want to put too big a dent in your post prandial drinks budget, this is a refreshing alternative to a fish supper. Ostensibly Persian cuisine but, in effect, a wide range of freshly made kebabs in generous naan bread, served up in slightly rough and ready, but convivial, surroundings. And change out of €10.

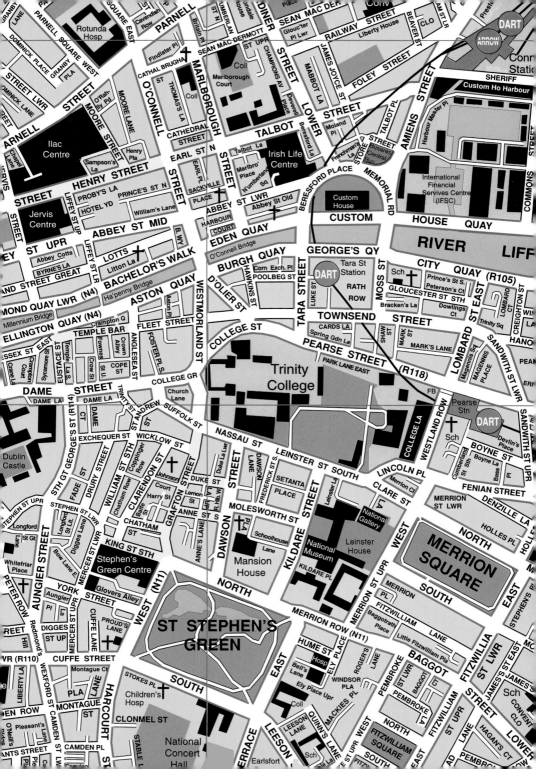

ISBN 1-872600-73-5

9 781872 600734 >

Price €6.99